PEDAL FORWARD

PEDAL FORWARD

The 10 Life And Business Lessons
I Have Learned On My Bike

TREY HALL

Pedal Forward: The 10 Life And Business Lessons I Have Learned On My Bike

Cairn Publishing Denver LLC, Denver 80202

© 2013, Trey Hall

All rights reserved. Published 2013.

Editing and production by Indigo Editing & Publications.

21 20 19 18 17 16 15 14 13   1 2 3 4 5

ISBN: 978-0-9893554-0-7
Library of Congress Control Number: 2013938820

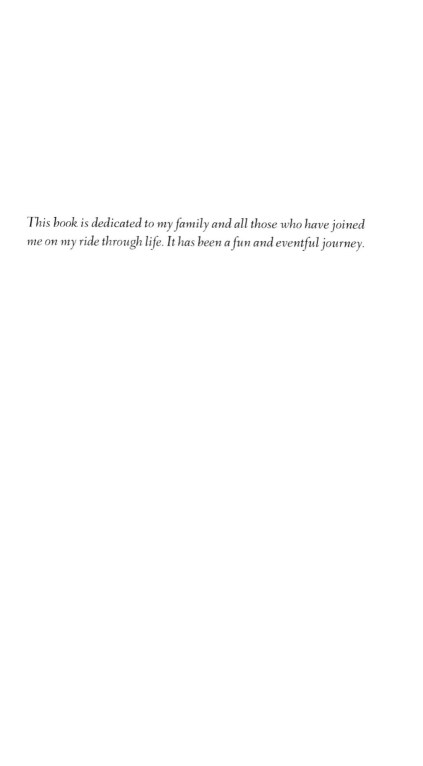

This book is dedicated to my family and all those who have joined me on my ride through life. It has been a fun and eventful journey.

Contents

Acknowledgments

I am eternally grateful to my wife, Ann, and my children, Ryan and Dallin, for their love. I am also extremely grateful for Ken Calwell, with whom I spent many hours sharing intense pain, amazing laughter, and unfailing encouragement to heal and move on with our lives.

I am also grateful for riding buddies who, over the years, have pulled and pushed me through epic rides in the Rockies and downright awful rides in places like Wichita Falls for the Hotter'N Hell Hundred. Chief among these riding buddies are John Lauck, Paul Kershisnik, and Carl Miller, but there are so many more.

I am also grateful for an amazing friend and coach, Arjun Sen, who encouraged me to write a book about my experiences.

Lastly, I would like to acknowledge the many colleagues who I have worked for and with during the first twenty-five years of my career. I have been blessed to work with some amazing people.

Foreword

If you choose to ride a bike, you will fall. We all learn this the first time we try to ride a bike. The question is not whether or not we will fall; the only real question is what we choose to do after we fall. That choice is our defining moment.

It was Thursday, August 8, 1991, at 6:40 a.m. on a two-lane road called Greenwich Road, just south and east of Wichita, Kansas. My friend Trey Hall and I will never forget our defining moment. We forget names, dates, phone numbers, and new passwords within minutes of learning them. However, twenty-plus years after our defining moment, we both remember it as if it happened today. Our defining moment did not happen while we were on our bikes; our defining moment did not even happen when we were knocked off our bikes.

If it were, then this book would be all about the details of this car–bike collision. The truth is that Trey spends only four pages of his nearly two-hundred-page book on the collision itself. Why? The collision is not the story. The collision was not our defining moment. Our defining moment was the decision we made *after* the collision. Our decision was to not be defined by the car-bike head-on collision, but instead to be *refined* through the lessons learned on our long journey to get back on our bikes and ride again. Trey shares in this book the ten lessons learned in that journey.

This book is for anyone who has ever faced—or collided with—a challenge. Our challenge was a 1978 Oldsmobile Cutlass crossing the centerline of a highway. Your challenge might be the loss of your health, a job, your spouse, your child, or another loved one. In this world we will all face challenges. Some seem to come out of nowhere, cross the center line, and strike us head-on when we least expect it. What I try to remember at these times is that challenge and trouble are an expected part of this fallen world that we live in.

In John 16:33 Jesus Christ says: "In this world you will have trouble." While that is a challenging verse to hear, I take great comfort in knowing this truth and in the words that Jesus says next: "In this world you will have trouble, but take heart, for I have overcome the world." What comfort and peace I have through my faith in Jesus, our Savior, who has overcome this fallen, troubled, and challenging world.

There is no question that we will face challenges in this world. The key question, our defining moment, arises when the inevitable challenge comes; it asks whether we will choose to be defined by the challenge or whether we will choose to be refined by the lessons learned from the challenge. Will we be defined by the challenge we face or be refined by it?

Defined versus refined: a single letter makes all the difference. Defined versus refined: the difference is simple.

The difference is whether the challenge in our life is our end point or our starting point. I have found that those who are defined by challenge in their lives chose to make the challenge the end point. They are defined by the challenge. These people focus on the past and talk in compromised terms and excuses of what could have, would have, or should have been had the challenge, or collision, in their life never occurred.

However, those who are refined by the challenges of life choose to accept the simple truth that the challenge is real and it happened. They realize that there is nothing they can do to change the past. It's about focus. Those who are refined, versus defined, by challenge are those who are able to focus 100 percent of their energy and effort on the future, using the challenge in their life as the starting point, not the end point.

The challenges we face in this world are not the end; they are merely the starting point of the journey. They are here to refine us, to make us stronger in our faith and more useful in our service to God, our family, and others in need. By looking at challenges in this world as the starting point in our journey of refinement, our challenges, hardships, and sufferings now have purpose. They serve to refine us, humble us, and make us more useful. Romans 5:3–5 says, "We are to rejoice in our sufferings because suffering produces perseverance, perseverance produces character, character produces hope, and hope does not disappoint us, because God has poured out his love into our hearts through the Holy Spirit that he has given us."

Trey and I first became acquainted as coworkers at the Pizza Hut corporate office. We became friends during the miles we covered together on our bikes, but we became lifetime friends by choosing to be refined, not defined, by the challenge we faced and overcame.

I love the promise God makes to us in Psalm 66:

Say to God, "How awesome are your deeds! Come and see what God has done, how awesome his works on our behalf. For you God tested us, you refined us like silver. Come and listen, let me tell you what God has done for me....God let men ride over our heads, we went through fire and water, but God brought us to a place of abundance. I cried out to God with my mouth (in prayer). God has surely listened and heard my voice in prayer. Praise be to God, who has heard my prayer and shared his love with me!

Thanks to God's love, grace, and answers to many prayers, Trey and I were not defined by our head-on collision with a car on the morning of August 8, 1991. God used that head-on collision as a starting point to refine us so that we could be more useful to him.

Thanks to God's refining process through our accident, I believe God has strengthened my faith. He has also built and refined Trey and me into better husbands, better fathers, better leaders, and better servants to those in need, and he continues to refine us day by day.

In this book, Trey continues his service to others by sharing wisdom learned one pedal stroke at a time as he went from lying on his back on the asphalt of a two-lane road in Wichita, to fighting for his life, to getting back on his bike, to continuing his journey.

Thank you, Trey, for your friendship. I look forward to our future rides together.

Ken Calwell
President and CEO, Papa Murphy's

Preface
Inspiration at the Dumpster Corral

I have had a long and meaningful relationship with bicycles. There has been a bike in my life in one way or another for most of my fifty-two years. Like most of us, my first bike provided me a sense of freedom and adventure. My bike was transportation to a life independent from my parents. It was a vehicle I used to see things and to be an adventurer, expanding my world from the end of the street to the vacant lot two blocks over, where I could join the other kids playing army, and to the corner market, where I could now buy candy without having to take a torturous hike to get there.

My first bike showed up unannounced. It wasn't my birthday; it wasn't any day special. But it ended up being my bike day. My dad showed up with it after work. It was a beautiful blue Schwinn with a coaster brake and training wheels. Since then my bike résumé has grown. It later included a really cool green Schwinn five-speed Stingray with a banana seat and tall handlebars with a car-like shifter. My bikes today are a little different: a dual-suspension carbon fiber Ibis Mojo and a carbon fiber–everything Pinnarello road bike.

As I grew older, the bike became less about transportation (I had a car to take me places) and more about an escape from an overscheduled life. Today when I ride my bike, not only do I feel the wind in my face, just like I did as a child, but I also get to exorcise the demons of adulthood and release the toxins of a demanding world. Riding also allows me to ponder the great things in my life, from my family to my job and the wonderful beauty that surrounds me.

When I am on my bike with a group, all the problems of the world fade as I revel in the power of group effort. When I am alone, I talk through problems and assemble solutions. When I am riding through rain, snow, or searing heat, I embrace the challenge and believe that, by enduring the pain, I am gaining a competitive advantage. Riding my bike has also created lasting friendships and a feeling of camaraderie.

Riding my bike has accompanied me through most of my college life and professional career. Riding became transportation again during college, when I attended Brigham Young University as an undergraduate and then later at Northwestern University, where I received my master's degree.

As I began my career at Foote, Cone & Belding (a large advertising agency), I discovered the therapeutic benefits of the bike as I rode through the idyllic north shore suburbs of Chicago. The bike bug followed my growing family and me to Southern California and then to Wichita, Kansas, where I worked for PepsiCo's Pizza Hut corporate office and where the bike flame was tended to a roaring fire.

It was in Wichita where my lessons on life and business and their connection to the bike really began. It was in Wichita, on August 8, 1991, that my good friend Ken Calwell and I were on our bikes during a training ride when a sleepy driver struck us head-on at 110 feet per second. The damage to our bodies was devastating.

Although both our bikes and bodies were crushed that morning, our desire to get back on our bikes was not. We had an obligation to ourselves and to everyone who loved us to get back on our bikes and thrive.

Both Ken and I have thrived.

We both were able to attain senior marketing positions within Pizza Hut. I then became the chief marketing officer, and later the chief brand officer, for Boston Market. I was the CMO for Quiznos twice (which shows my reluctance to leave Colorado, where both these great organizations are headquartered), the first CMO for Smashburger, the philanthropic head of Consumer Capital Partners private equity firm, and the global CMO for the iconic TGI Friday's. Ken is now the president and chief executive officer of Papa Murphy's.

Over the course of this career progression, I kept riding my bike. I fell off a few more times. I saw others crash. I had other mishaps and adventures. All of these experiences created a connection between bike riding and key lessons, which I began to share with my children and friends.

I started thinking about writing this book during my second tenure at Boston Market way back in 2001. I had a nice corner office that had a dramatic view looking east into the plains that surround Denver, and closer up, I had a direct view of the Dumpster. I think they called it the Dumpster corral because there were actually several Dumpsters, and it was a very active place. The Boston Market test kitchen folks used it with great frequency. I recall sitting at my desk one evening, as the afternoon shadows were lengthening into night, and contemplating some of the business challenges I faced. As I was deep in thought, movement below me brought my attention to the Dumpster corral, as much of the day's test kitchen labor was being tossed into the dirty, nasty container. I focused there for a moment and then had the good fortune to look up.

Darkness had fully enveloped the day, and the twinkle of lights began to appear. I could see the glow of Denver International Airport in the far distance. This beauty—the lights from the eastern plains, the glow of the distant airport, and the twinkling of downtown Denver—pulled my thoughts from the Dumpster and focused them on a grander place.

It was then—and I am not making this up simply because it sounds good at the start of the book—that the thought of developing something of potential worth to leave to my family and hopefully others began to take shape. I wanted to leave a legacy that was more than the observations of a Dumpster corral. I wanted to leave thoughts that had the potential to teach and lift—and perhaps even inspire like the lights over the eastern plains of Colorado.

Over the ensuing weeks, I took notes when inspiration would strike, and slowly lessons formed.

The bike connection was organic. The bike had become who I was, so it naturally became part of the fabric of the lessons I would pass on. I shared the lessons with some friends. Some they liked; others they did not. After extensive editing, I had thirteen lessons that I was fired up about. Over the next several years, I would write a little bit here and there, with the contents of this book slowly taking shape.

When it came time to get really serious, thirteen lessons condensed to ten. I like to think all ten of these lessons have one common trait. Some are more explicitly tied in to it than others, but they all strive to teach one basic idea:

We have an amazing soul that is tougher than we think, is more compassionate than we believe, and whose true north points toward goodness and joy. In a world that will knock us off our bikes, we must be resolute in getting back on (no matter how many times we get knocked off). We have to find

joy in the journey even while we are pushing ourselves—
sometimes beyond reason. We have to learn to become
good citizens, sharing what we know with clarity and good
character. We are here to enjoy the ride. Sometimes that
takes a lot of work, but it sure beats being miserable.

As mentioned, I wrote this more for me and my progeny than
for anyone else. I hope that they will find some direction in these
lessons over the years. I hope others can also find some direction
in them.

I'd like the final words of this preface to come from someone
far wiser than I:

I sought my God and my God I could not find.
I sought my soul and my soul eluded me.
I sought my brother to serve him in his need,
And I found all three—my God, my soul, and thee.
—Anonymous

It has been more than twenty years since that defining accident knocked me off my bike and bloodied me a bit. The lessons
learned that day and since have helped me to overcome the trials
and to revel in the joys of my life.

I am still on the bike nearly every day. Whether you ride or not,
I hope you enjoy reading about what I have learned.

Part I

The Big Crash

Blood, Guts, and a 1978 Olds Cutlass

On this particular morning of this particular day, nearly everyone in our cycling group was traveling. We all worked at the Pizza Hut corporate headquarters, and usually there were six to ten of us in our group. But on the morning of August 8, 1991, luckily there were only two of us who met at the Dillons grocery store parking lot: my good friend and office neighbor Ken Calwell, and me.

It was fairly typical Wichita August morning—hot and humid, even at six a.m. The sun was just rising, and the sky was a steel gray. The humidity in Wichita never allowed for deep blue skies, something my wife and I didn't miss when we later moved to Colorado. Instead, the sky was always a hazy gray, just as it was this morning. The wind was coming from the south at about ten miles per hour (we didn't have mountains in Wichita, but we did have wind), so we would typically head into the wind for the first leg of the ride and then turn to have a joyous downwind run all the way home.

That was going to be the case this particular morning. Ken and I would ride south on Greenwich Road about twelve miles and then turn around where Greenwich dead-ended and head home. In the Dillons supermarket parking lot, Ken mentioned that he wasn't feeling great. He wondered if I would pull—in bike terms, this means riding in front so the other riders can draft—for the first few miles until he started to feel better.

We took off with me pulling Ken. As we approached Greenwich Road, I glanced at my watch—6:20 a.m. We pedaled south, past the mammoth Boeing Field assembly plant on the east side of the street. The facility was huge, and we rode along the boundary fence for about three miles. Just past the Boeing field, about a mile west, was where our Pizza Hut headquarters was located. As we rode by, I glanced in the direction of our offices, and the day's long list of tasks started to invade my head: lots of emails to return, several important meetings to lead, preparations to be made for one of our agency partners who was flying in from Miami to present some work. I pushed them out of my mind. I was riding my bike, and I needed to focus. Work would come later, and because of this ride, I would be better at it. The endorphins from the morning would propel me through the day.

I cleared my head and concentrated on the road whirling beneath my spinning tires. A mile farther up the road, we came to the corner of Greenwich Road and Kellogg, the main thoroughfare through Wichita. At this time the corner represented the border of urban development. Beyond this corner, everything was still very much country: lots of wheat fields with just a few farmhouses here and there.

We powered through the intersection into the vast Kansas farmland, where Greenwich Road narrowed to two lanes and a six-inch shoulder identified with a recently painted white ribbon. On either side of the road was a barrow ditch, which collected all the water when it rained. It was a couple feet deep, and you didn't want to run off the road on your bike and end up in there. It was never pretty when you did. I'd had several experiences with it. The good news for me was I had mountain biking experience and could usually ride it out without crashing. Many others were not as lucky and either went over their handlebars or otherwise crashed.

The speed limit on the road was 55 miles per hour with stop signs breaking the rhythm of the ride every two miles. The road was as straight as an arrow, and the asphalt was relatively smooth for a road that was essentially in the middle of nowhere. We chose this road for its smooth asphalt and its lack of traffic.

As we crossed the boundary from urban to country, which we did every morning, I looked over at the fire station on our left and saw some activity there. We headed under the overpass that carried the trains into downtown Wichita, and we welcomed the cooler air the bridge offered, even this early in the morning.

We were about five miles into the ride at this point. Ken started to feel better, so he began to pull. The wind was smack in our faces, blowing directly from the south. We had been riding at about 20 miles per hour into the wind, and Ken maintained that speed as he took the lead.

I fell into rhythm behind him. Whenever I was drafting, I kept my front wheel about six inches off his back wheel to maintain the most advantageous position. To maintain that distance, I counted on Ken—or whomever was pulling—to ride at a consistent speed and use hand signals to let me know what was approaching or if he was slowing down. Otherwise, those six inches closed way too fast and bad things could happen. My eyes were affixed to his seat post, my hands in the handlebar drops with my fingers lightly touching the brake levers. I did not dare do too much sightseeing in this position. A bad move on my part could send me crashing into his back wheel and bring us both down. I was in this position when we approached a point about a mile and a half from the intersection of Greenwich and Kellogg.

Mulvane is a sleepy little town about fifteen miles south of Wichita. It is an agricultural community surrounded by farms. Many of its population commute into Wichita for jobs in the aeronautical industry, which for the most part keeps Wichita surviving. Companies like Boeing, Cessna, and Learjet all have large manufacturing facilities located on the east side of Wichita.

Mulvane is the home of a woman who, for the sake of anonymity, I will call Karen. In writing this book and relating the story of the accident in particular, I debated if I should identify the antagonist. During a discussion with Ken Calwell when I was checking my facts with his, we debated using the driver's real name. We concluded that it served no real purpose, that we all make mistakes, and that no positive outcome would come from naming her. So she will be dubbed Karen (apologies to all the Karens out there).

Karen worked at Cessna Aircraft as a riveter. She lived in a trailer with her disabled husband on property that was littered with debris, broken-down cars, and trash. The property was overgrown and relatively hidden in this tiny town tucked away in the wheat fields of south central Kansas. Every morning at dawn, Karen would get into her 1978 Olds Cutlass and drive to her job. After several turns along dusty country roads, she would turn onto Greenwich Road and head north to the Cessna factory.

Karen had a medical condition called narcolepsy. Her condition was known only to her, her doctor, her husband, and a few others. Narcolepsy causes those who are affected to fall asleep without warning. It doesn't matter what those people may be doing—riveting bolts onto an airplane or driving a car—they simply nod off. Karen knew that she probably should not be driving, but since her doctor never explicitly told her not to drive, she figured she could ignore her common sense.

This morning, Karen was having a tough time. She was foggy and knew her narcolepsy was a bigger problem than usual. Despite these concerns, she got into her car and headed for work. At 6:35 a.m. she began to weave down Greenwich Road, falling asleep and then waking up again. She kept driving north. She needed to get to work.

At 6:40, Karen blew through a stop sign about four miles from the intersection of Greenwich and Kellogg.

She was asleep.

She awoke in time to correct the car from driving left of center, only to fall asleep again. Her Olds Cutlass was traveling at about 55 miles per hour. As she fell asleep a third time, she slumped against the steering wheel, pushing the car across the center line and toward Ken and me riding south on the west shoulder at about 20 miles per hour.

Physics would tell you that the closing speed of the car and our two bikes was about 75 miles per hour—about 110 feet per second. There was no time to react. Ken was not looking for a car coming into our lane. He was concentrating on keeping a smooth cadence. Ken did not see the car coming until it crossed the centerline. I don't recall the approach of the car at all. I was focused on his seat post—I didn't want to make us crash.

My only recollection of the actual impact was a sudden jerking sensation followed by a sense of falling. The falling feeling was due to my sailing over the car. I don't recall the landing. Thankfully.

Obviously the car had struck Ken first. His impact point was right between the headlights in the center of the car's grille. The car, as it struck Ken, was at a slight angle. As you can imagine, at that speed the force of the impact was brutal. Ken's aluminum bike flattened against the grille, exploding into thirty-eight pieces (we counted them). The twisting angle of the car and the force of the impact sent Ken from the grille and into the windshield. This in turn twisted his body and sent him careening off the windshield and under the car, where the back right wheel ran over him and spit him out. Ken's body was a broken and bloody mess. He was left lying on his back with his legs facing east and his head west. His head was about a foot from the right edge of the road.

In the milliseconds it took the car to get to me, it had straightened out a bit. I too struck the car in the now-damaged grille right between the two headlights. The first part of my body to strike the car was my left hand, which was still in the drop of the handlebar. Second was my left knee, which was at the highest point of the pedal rotation. Both my hand and knee exploded on impact. The rest of my body followed as the bike accordioned into the grille, driving up through my body and into my pelvis, which broke. I flew into the windshield, with my right cheek leading the way. My torso followed, bending at the waist (not in its natural forward bend but in the completely unnatural backward way), breaking and dislocating six vertebrae as it bent. This in turn sent me onto the roof of the car, which acted as a trampoline and vaulted me high into the air. I landed on my left side just a few feet from Ken. My head faced east, my legs west. I was nearly perpendicular to the middle stripe of the road.

Ken and I were both conscious. We had some very serious, nearly mortal wounds. They hurt. They hurt a lot. I don't recall any sharp pains at that time but rather a deep, dull, searing, penetrating pain. I liken it to when you skin your knee and you feel a burning sensation. I felt that sensation, and it was all over my body multiplied by a significant amount. I also felt wet and sticky. The blood that poured from our bodies mingled with our sweat and the road dirt, coating us.

Not surprisingly, Karen woke up sometime during the crash, as I am sure we made quite a racket slamming into her car. Her car ended up in the barrow ditch—that place you never want to be.

We totaled the Cutlass. The front end of the car was mangled, the windshield was caved in and broken to bits, the hood was dented and scratched, and the roof was pushed in.

The car was a mess and so was Karen. As she emerged, she walked around the back of the car to see the devastation she had leveled. She began to scream. Karen was hysterical. She was screaming and asking if we were hurt.

We were.

I recall asking her what time it was. For some reason it was important to me. Karen told me it was about six forty a.m. I then asked if this was real and not a dream. She screeched in anguish that it was real and that I was bleeding badly. I figured as much, but I didn't look. My eyes were clinched shut. I did not want to see. The pain was penetrating.

While I think I knew I was badly hurt, part of my mind was being optimistic. I was thinking, *Well, it's now six forty. It's going to take me some time to get my breath back and stand up. If my bike is broken, then I'll probably have to find a ride home somehow. Dang, I'll probably be late to work.*

I began to panic a bit. Some of my meetings could be rearranged, and emails could be pounded out at home, but what was I going to do about the agency that had flown all the way from Miami to meet with me? I needed to get ahold of them and somehow explain that I was going to be late. I hate being late.

In the midst of this nonsense, I heard Ken calling my name.

"Trey," he said.

I replied, "What?"

"Is that your foot behind my head?"

With my eyes still clinched shut, I said, "Ken, if it is my foot, we're in a lot more trouble than I'm hoping we're in."

I heard a grunt from Ken as he lay on his back and strained to look over his right shoulder to see what his head was resting on.

I heard him utter, "Oh my. That's my foot." He recognized the socks he had put on that morning.

This is a good point in the story (before the paramedics arrive) to share the rundown on the injuries. I'll share them in rather a blunt, unemotional way. I don't mean to, really, but over the years it has become just a list to me. It is still a painful list, but a list nonetheless.

Ken
- *Concussion. His helmet was in five pieces.*
- *Two open compound fractures of the right lower arm.*
- *Two fractures of the upper right arm.*
- *Severe nerve damage to the right shoulder and arm that allowed no use of these extremities.*
- *Lacerations and nerve damage around the right eye socket.*
- *Compound fracture of the right leg (femur). This was the leg that was bent around backward with his foot lying beneath his head.*
- *Three compound and open fractures of the left leg (tibia/fibula) and one simple fracture.*
- *Three fractures of the pelvis.*
- *Significant blood loss.*
- *Road rash literally from head to toe, with severe lacerations and open wounds requiring multiple skin grafts, hundreds of stitches, and staples.*
- *PCL tear in the right knee.*

Me
- *Two fractures of the pelvis.*
- *Six broken and dislocated vertebrae.*
- *A nearly severed right foot held to my body by only the Achilles tendon.*

- *A complete dislocation of the left knee that included an open compound fracture of the left patella and complete tears of the PCL, patella tendon, and both the medial and lateral collateral tendons. My lower leg was literally hanging by the skin surrounding what remained of my knee.*
- *ACL tear of the right knee.*
- *Collapsed left lung, with the right one working on half volume.*
- *A left hand split in two pieces.*
- *An open compound fracture of the left elbow.*
- *Significant blood loss.*
- *Road rash, lacerations, and open wounds literally from head to toe.*

We were both in big trouble. Ken had much more bone trauma; I had more soft tissue trauma. We were both lying on Greenwich Road dying.

We didn't die, though. We gave ourselves a chance to survive. Because we trained hard, our hearts were in good shape. When we stopped riding and lay down, like we were doing in the middle of Greenwich Road, our heart rates slowed, which slowed the blood being pumped out of our damaged bodies.

Of the many miracles that kept us alive that day, this was the first. We did not bleed to death. We were in great shape, and that gave us a chance to survive.

The next miracle occurred in the form of a nurse. She was following Karen and had watched her weave down the road. She watched as she crossed the centerline of Greenwich Road and hit what she thought at the time was trash bags because of how high the two objects flew into the air. When she realized we were not trash bags, she stopped, assessed the situation, got back in her car, and raced to the fire station at the corner of Greenwich and Kellogg that Ken and I had passed earlier in our ride. This was before the time of cell phones, and she realized very quickly that on this sparsely traveled road, the best thing she could do for us was get us help as quickly as possible, not stop and try to stem the massive bleeding that both Ken and I had. There was no way she could have done it. Our best chance for survival was to get fully equipped EMTs to our aid.

The third miracle occurred when the nurse arrived at the fire station. There was a shift change happening, so two teams were standing around the firehouse. Both teams mobilized to come take care of us. One team focused on Ken, the other on me. If it were not for the two teams, we are convinced that one or both of us would have died because of lack of focus, lack of hands.

The fourth miracle occurred because on this day, the paramedics were testing compression pants. These special pants, when inflated, helped stem the bleeding in our lower extremities. If they had not had access to these compression pants, they would have had to use tourniquets to stop the bleeding. The use of tourniquets has serious implications, including the possible loss of the limbs. These pants helped us survive, and once we did, helped us have lives that are full and active.

Paramedics and firemen are my heroes. They arrived quickly on the scene of the accident and saw a grim situation. Karen was still screaming as Ken and I were lying in the road pumping out huge quantities of blood. Later, one of the paramedics described us as the bugs that get squished on your windshield, except that we were still alive and we talked back. The scene so unnerved one of the paramedics that he later quit and found new work. They literally had to scoop our parts off the pavement and stick them into the compression pants.

While I never saw the paramedics—I kept my eyes closed due to the pain—I recall the conversations with them very clearly. One of these conversations is the fifth miracle. I recall one of the firemen sitting down next to me to keep me awake and talking while also asking questions about how to contact my family. I clearly remember his asking for my wife's name. I told him. He asked for my phone number, which I gave him, but then I added that no one was home but the dog and that my family was in Hawaii (Ann took the boys home every summer to visit her folks). What happened next still astounds me. Very clearly and calmly and with no hesitation, I was able to give him my in-laws' names, their street address, the town, the island, and their phone number. To this point, and at any point after this incident, I would never have been able to do this. As anyone who is married can attest, memorizing your in-laws' important information is not high on the list of things to keep in your brain.

What is also interesting was what was important to me at this time. I had gotten over that I probably wasn't going to get to work on time, but I began to panic a bit about the dog. I told the fireman that I had a potential problem at home. He asked what it was, and I said I needed to get home to let the dog out and feed her breakfast. I didn't want to come home and have dog poop all over the house. He asked what kind of dog it was—she was a black lab—and what her name was—Mali. He then asked me how to get into the house. I had left the front door unlocked.

Later he and the rest of the firemen and their big red truck went to the grocery store, bought dog food (I had not told him where the food was), and went to my house. They took Mali for a walk and fed her. They continued to check on Mali and feed her until Ann got home later that day and organized the situation. To me this was as heroic and human-defining as saving my life.

The sixth miracle occurred when we got to the hospital. There was a trauma team shift change occurring, which once again meant there were two dedicated teams—one to work on Ken, the other on me. Part of this miracle was that the trauma doc assigned to me was the father of a woman who worked for me. I had been to his house out in the country to train Mali.

The rest of my early ER memories are scattered. I do recall getting sick and throwing up in the MRI tube. I remember how ridiculous it

sounded to me when the MRI technician asked me to hold my breath when I was in the tube—I couldn't breathe anyway.

At some point in the ER, they cut me open and stuck tubes down into my collapsed lungs and began to pump them back up. I'm glad I don't remember. Much later, I do remember them taking the tubes out. I could feel them slide from way inside me out through the hole they had cut in me. It was slow, and while it didn't really hurt, it was an amazingly weird sensation.

Trey Hall [left] and Ken Calwell [right] six months after the accident. This photograph was used in an ad campaign for the rehab unit at St. Joseph's Hospital in Wichita, Kansas. There are two bikes in the pile of wreckage below us.

The seventh miracle manifested in the abilities of the surgeons who worked on me. I was in surgery from nine a.m. or so until about five p.m.—a real marathon. They first stabilized my back by installing Harrington rods. These titanium implements were anchored into my pelvis and wired along my spine up to just under my shoulder blades. The surgeons essentially glued my pelvis back together at the same time. They then worked on cleaning out and suturing all my open wounds on the top half of my body. They then somehow rotated me and began working on my left arm's compound fracture, my left hand issues, my left knee, and right (almost) severed foot. It was an amazing feat. The surgeons, led by orthopedist Dr. Robert Eyster, did an amazing job. They left my right knee for another time, but the work they did is still working to this day.

The most important miracle was Ann. After she got the phone call from the hospital, Ann began arranging for her travel home. She had gone to Hawaii on some cheap tickets, so her return was no easy matter, and with two young boys, it became an even bigger ordeal. The first flights out of Hawaii are typically not until eleven a.m. or so, which gave her a lot of time to worry. Her flight home took her from Honolulu to Los Angeles. From Los Angeles, she and the boys flew to Las Vegas for a layover in the casino disguised as an airport. After a rather lengthy stay in Vegas, where our youngest son, Dallin, rolled on the floor underneath the slot machines, she got back on another plane and flew to Colorado Springs for yet another layover. Finally, from Colorado Springs she flew to Wichita, arriving in the middle of the evening, after I had gotten out of surgery and recovery.

Although I was very foggy, I remember her coming into my SICU (surgical intensive care unit) room. I had been very anxious to see her. Once she got there, I remember relaxing and being able to sleep. Ann stayed with me that night and slept on the hard, cold floor next to my bed. Throughout her travel ordeal, she called the hospital during each layover to check on the status of my surgery.

It was in the second day after the accident (when I was a little more coherent—or maybe not) that I concluded I probably wouldn't make it back to work until Monday. I had been holding out hope that although I was hurt, perhaps the weekend would allow me some time to heal and that I'd be able to get back to work after two restful days. Clearly that did not happen. I was in ICSU for a couple of weeks. I was not back to work for many, many months.

Ken was in surgery at least as long as I was, and when we came out, we were both in ICSU. He eventually had more surgeries than I did.

During our daylong surgeries and in the days that followed, our friends from Pizza Hut gathered at the hospital. So many came that the administrators at the hospital thought they had some kind of celebrity rock stars recovering at their hospital. We were far from rock stars, but we had some incredible support.

My assistant and the account executive from Pizza Hut's local advertising agency organized the troops. Later, when we were out of ICSU and into the regular hospital, they set up a visitation schedule to manage the number of visitors we had. They also sent out daily updates on our condition. At times the reports were a little ambitious and shared a little too much. But there was love in the updates, and the reports made it all over the country, and even internationally, as the Pizza Hut family wanted to know how we were doing. I found it amazing that so many people cared. Ken and I were not notable in any real respect, but I like to think we were nice to people and worked hard, and others appreciated that.

There it is, the story that started it all. But like all stories, there is a backstory, and in this case, I think it is important to tell for context.

The Wichita Backstory

My family and I had moved to Wichita in early 1990 to lead sports marketing for Pizza Hut, part of the PepsiCo empire at that time. Life was awesome; I was brought in to manage the company's interest in the NCAA and Little League and later, at the time of the accident, the advertising efforts for the whole chain. Ann, my wife, and I had two young growing sons: Ryan, who was six, and Dallin, who was just about two years old on August 8. We lived in the kind of house we had always dreamed of. We had many wonderful friends. Life was really good.

In Wichita, the guys I wanted to associate with were all into cycling. I had begun to ride regularly when we lived in Chicago and later in California. Ann had bought me a bike, and over the years and through our moves, I had used it with some regularity. But in Wichita, with limited recreational opportunities, cycling seemed like a fun thing to get serious about, and my friends were all into it. So I went to a local Wichita bike shop and bought a new Trek road bike.

My first ride with the guys was a long one and felt like it would nearly kill me, but it gave me the bug for serious riding. Cycling held some of the same attributes that skiing did for me—freedom, the wind in your hair, and as much as all that, the camaraderie. In both skiing and cycling, there is fun in numbers.

After recovering from my first ride, I began riding every morning before work with these same friends. Some mornings there would be a big group, other mornings just a small group, but every morning I came away from the ride with an endorphin rush that would propel me through the day.

Two guys were the most dedicated: John Lauck and Paul Kershisnik. They rode every morning, rain or shine. I decided that I would be as committed, and I rode with them each morning, even those mornings that were bitterly cold. At first I could only stay with them for a portion of the ride. We generally did out-and-back rides, and I would hang with them for as long as I could on the out portion of the ride. Eventually I would lose contact but would keep riding until they made the turn. When I saw them, I would turn and ride back with them. There came a day, and I still remember it as an overcast morning, when I was able to keep up with them all the way out and all the way back. It was a real adrenalin rush for me.

I progressed in my fitness quickly and enjoyed getting involved in the Wichita cycling community. We became staples at the bike shop and even got Pizza Hut to sponsor the shop's team, which we of course became a part of.

I also began to look at sponsorships for Pizza Hut on the national stage. I went to Colorado Springs to meet with the United States Cycling Federation (now USA Cycling). I met with the head of the organization, and we brainstormed ways that we might make a sponsorship work. They also took me to the US Olympic Training Center Velodrome with one of their coaches and taught me how to ride on the track. They gave me official USA Team cycling clothes—including shoes—and I rode the bike that had won the national championship. It was an incredible experience that galvanized my love for the sport.

This leads to the ten life and business lessons I have learned as I have pedaled my bike—up and down big hills, riding with big friendly groups and small, more intimate ones. I had that run-in with a 1978 Olds Cutlass driven by a sleepy lady from Mulvane, Kansas, and as you'll read, you'll hear tales of snow and close calls with lightning and bears. I have fallen off my bike more than once, but each time I have gotten back on. I have experienced great joy on my bike. I have been in great pain both on and off my bike. Cycling has given me a great time to ponder the great opportunities I've been given and the lessons I've learned from them.

These lessons mean something to me. I hope you find meaning in them as well.

Part II

The Ten Life and Business Lessons I Have Learned on My Bike

Lesson 1
It's the After that Matters Most

Ken and I both fell off our bikes on August 8, 1991, with a little help from a 1978 Olds Cutlass. We hit the asphalt pretty hard. As we lay in the hospital, we made a resolution to get better. Our purpose was to do everything in our power to restore ourselves. We worked hard. We were focused and dedicated to our task. It was what we had been trained to do at work—when you fall down, you get up.

The fact is, if you ride a bike, you will fall off at one time or another. This is an inevitable truth—you will be dislodged from your road bike, your mountain bike, and even your Life Cycle at the club. What matters most is what you do after you fall off. What matters is how you respond to the adversity, how you make yourself better *after*.

In the summer of 2012, Ken had his fiftieth birthday, and his wife, Sandy, organized a surprise birthday party for him in beautiful Steamboat Springs, Colorado. Cody Barnett, Ken's physical therapist during our recovery, made the long drive from Kansas to attend the party.

At the time of recovery, Cody was fresh out of school, a young kid with very little experience but a huge amount of compassion and perhaps an even bigger desire to help people.

Cody used some rather unorthodox rehab techniques to help Ken. One night recently, as we were sitting around talking about

the old days, Cody made a very interesting comment about work ethic and what he experienced with Ken during his rehabilitation. Cody mentioned that in the twenty years since the accident, he has never ever had a patient work as hard as Ken (I like to think I worked hard too, but I wasn't his patient). No patient has pushed so hard, asked as many questions, and been as driven to get better as Ken was. Cody mentioned that in many ways, it has been disappointing to him that others who have fallen off their bikes have not

Trey Hall [left] and Ken Calwell [right] at Ken's fiftieth surprise birthday party held in Steamboat Springs, Colorado—twenty-one years after the accident.

wanted to get back on with the intensity that Ken did.

I think the lesson is pretty simple, really. When you fall off your bike (and you will, no matter what you choose to do in life), you get back on and ride even harder. You learn from the pain. You give the fall purpose. You don't waste the experience. You want to be compared to Ken Calwell, not one of Cody's other patients. It is really the after that matters.

One other quick story to illustrate this principle from a slightly different angle involves my son Ryan when he was just learning to ride his bike at about four years old. In our family lore we call this story "The High-Speed Wobbles":

Ryan was adventurous. From an early age, he liked to do things that gave him a thrill. At the swimming pool, he loved to be thrown as far as I could toss him from the edge into the water. I was young and he was small, so I could throw him a long way. He loved it.

The same was true with his bike. He wanted to learn to ride so he could have some freedom and go fast. We bought him a little second-hand, black, off-road bike with knobby tires. It had training wheels at first, but he quickly mastered his balance, and they soon came off.

> Our greatest glory is not in never falling but in rising every time we fall.
>
> —CONFUCIUS

One of the great joys of our family weekends was going on walks through our neighborhood and dreaming of one day being able to afford a real house, not just our condo. On these walks, Ryan would ride his bike. It wasn't hard to keep up.

One particular Saturday afternoon, Ryan wanted to go for a ride. Ann was occupied with something, so I volunteered to take him. I really enjoyed our walks and talking to Ryan in this casual setting. It became the basis for my interviews with our kids in the future—the conversations I had with the boys were always best accomplished playing catch, sitting on the ski lift, or riding our bikes. Anyway, as we were leaving, Ann admonished me not to let Ryan ride down any hills. She shared that he had been wanting to go faster than she was comfortable allowing, as she was worried that he still had not mastered the stopping skill. I assured her I would be mature and responsible, and we left the house.

I strapped on his helmet, popped him on the bike (he couldn't get on it by himself), gave him a push, and he was on his way. We had a great walk, winding through the houses and eucalyptus trees surrounding our condo complex. Ryan was riding great. He seemed to have great control of his bike. I was very proud.

Near our home was a hill. On our return, as we approached, Ryan asked if he could ride down it. Ann's parting words flashed through my head, but I countered those thoughts with the fact that Ryan was riding well and that he was controlling his bike like a pro. So we stopped at the top of the hill. I knelt down and asked him if he really knew how to use his brakes. In his innocent four-year-old way, he assured me that he did. I then told him he could ride down the hill, but only if he used the brakes the whole way down and didn't go too fast. He assured me he would. I straightened his helmet, gave him a little push to get him started, and away he went.

The first part of the trip down went well—he was clearly applying brakes, and his speed was in check. His guidance system also seemed to be working well. I jogged behind him. Things were looking good. I briefly thought that perhaps Ann was being overprotective.

Halfway down the hill, things started going bad. His little hands got tired of braking. He gained speed and began to outpace me. As the hill bottomed out, he had gained some good speed for a little guy, and the bike began to wobble—the high-speed wobbles. The high-speed wobbles have been known to take down even the most experienced speed demons, and Ryan fell victim to them. The wobbles became uncontrollable, and down he went. In reality he wasn't going very fast, and the hill really wasn't that long or steep, but he went down, and there was nothing I could do about it.

I arrived at the crash site literally moments after he hit the asphalt. He and the bike were mangled together. I carefully unwound the two of them. He wasn't skinned up badly at all. He wasn't crying, but he said his arm hurt. Scared and not wanting anything to be wrong, I said he would be okay and that he needed to get back on his bike and ride the rest of the way home. He agreed, so I placed him back on the bike, lifted the arm he was complaining about onto the bike grip, and gave him a little push to get started.

I walked beside him as we approached our condo. I got him off the bike and made him promise not to tell Mommy that he went down the hill and crashed. He agreed. Had I really thought Ann was being overprotective? I was very nervous. I was scared and cowardly. I didn't want anything to be wrong, because I did not want to face my wife. It was clearly my fault that Ryan was hurt.

Ann was in the kitchen as we entered the condo, said a fast hello, and then quickly went upstairs. We went straight to Ryan's room. He again said that his arm really hurt, so I took off his long-sleeved shirt to get a good look at the offending body part. On his left forearm there appeared to be a small joint that hadn't been there previously. This didn't look good on many levels. Ryan still was not crying, but I could tell he was really hurting. I steeled myself and went downstairs to tell Ann that Ryan was hurt. She came quickly upstairs, took one look at him, and off they went to the hospital. I don't recall being invited to go.

A couple hours later, they returned with Ryan's arm in a big temporary cast. An appointment with a pediatric orthopedist had been scheduled for Monday. It was clear I would be the one taking him to that appointment, as Ryan had spilled the beans that I had let him ride the bike down the hill.

On Monday I came home from work, picked up Ryan, and took him to the doctor. After the obligatory long wait, the nurse came out and asked to see Ryan. I got up with him but was invited to take a seat until the doctor called for me. I sat back down. The examination room was close to the waiting room, and the door was open when the doctor started questioning Ryan about his broken arm.

"How did you break your arm?" asked the doctor.

"My dad did it," Ryan answered.

"Your dad broke your arm?" the doctor asked.

Ryan said, "Yes. He let me ride down the hill that I wasn't sup-posed to, and I got the high-speed wobbles and crashed on my bike."

"Oh, I see," the doctor said.

I was then permitted to join the exam. Ryan's arm was set and put in a hot-pink cast of his choosing. I barely escaped a visit by social services.

Many times we create our own mishaps and fall off the bike, or in this case, our neglect causes others to suffer misfortune. When we find ourselves guilty of this behavior, what defines us is how we take accountability *after* the event.

> A duty dodged is like a debt unpaid: it is only deferred, and we must come back and settle the account at last.
>
> —JOSEPH FORT NEWTON

In the case of Ryan and the high-speed wobbles, I completely failed the after. I did not take accountability or ownership of my mistake. We owe it to ourselves and those around us to be immediately forthright, completely honest, and totally accountable. It's always difficult to admit a mistake, but those people we admire most over the course of history have been those who have risen from mistakes or misfortune to triumph, giving the mistake purpose. They triumphed in the after.

When you fall off your bike, no matter the circumstance, dust yourself off, take responsibility for it, and get back on. It's the after that matters most.

Lesson 2

Good and Bad: The Righteous Partnership

My time on and off the bike has taught me that there is an important alliance, a righteous partnership, between good and bad. One without the other would make an incredibly bleak canvas of our lives. We need the shadows to appreciate the highlights in a painting. We need the bad in life to appreciate the good.

After six months or so of surgeries and hospital stays after my run-in with the Cutlass, I got back to work. I had my last surgery on my right knee several weeks before I stepped into the Pizza Hut building to start working again. It was a great feeling to get back to my desk and be productive. It had been a long six months.

Not long after returning, I scheduled a meeting in New Orleans. I don't recall what the meeting was about or why I was going, but I remember I was in New Orleans when I awoke in the middle of the night with a high fever and severe nausea. Since my last surgery, I had not been feeling well, but I was just a little achy. The therapist and I thought it was fatigue, so we had pulled back on therapy a bit.

When I awoke during the night in New Orleans, along with the sweat and nausea, my right knee was really hurting. I turned on the nightstand light and pulled back the covers on the bed. What I saw made me even sicker. Over the course of a few hours, my knee had grown to about three times its normal size, stretching the skin so tight, I thought it might burst. My knee looked like a very big, painful pimple. It was the size of a grapefruit, and I couldn't bend it. Panic rushed over me.

I laid my head back on the pillow and contemplated what I needed to do. In a moment of brilliance, I determined I needed to see a doctor. In a moment of stupidity, I concluded I needed to see Dr. Eyster in Wichita. It never occurred to me that they had doctors in New Orleans.

I needed to get back to Wichita—and fast. At this early hour, I called the travel agent hotline and booked the first plane back to Wichita. There are, of course, no direct flights from anywhere to Wichita, so I had to make a connection through Dallas. This meant a long, arduous day of travel. I then called my business companions, waking them up, to tell them I was going home—something was wrong with me.

The travel day back to Wichita is a bit of a blur. I was sick and in a ton of pain. The pain and throbbing in my knee spread to my entire leg. The sweating and nausea also increased over the course of the day. When I finally got to Wichita, I was in bad shape. I had sweated through my clothes; I'm sure those around me on the plane thought I was an Ebola victim.

Once I was in Wichita, somehow I staggered to my Jeep, lugging my baggage. Even more amazing is that I was able to climb into the Jeep and use my swollen right leg to make it go and stop. In a daze, I managed to drive to Dr. Eyster's office next to St. Joe's hospital.

I had called the doctor's office before boarding one of my planes to let them know I was coming to visit and that something was wrong with my knee because it looked like a giant zit. I'm sure the nurse thought I was exaggerating because she said I "must have thrown a stitch." I had also called Ann and given her my story, a very mild version of the truth so she wouldn't worry. I asked her to meet me at the doctor's office and gave her the time I thought I would be there.

I pulled up to Dr. Eyster's office and parked half on the sidewalk, half in the street in a very illegal place. I left everything in the car and literally staggered to his office.

By this time I was a bit of a celebrity at the office. I never had to wait. When I walked in, the receptionist saw me coming and opened the door to the examination rooms. A nurse met me there and, with her usual cheeriness, said, "Let's see this knee."

At this stage of my recovery, I could drop my pants in front of anyone without much concern. I turned to face her, she shut the door, and down came my pants. I watched her face as she gazed down at my knee and now a very red, swollen leg. She had very little facial expression as she turned on her heels and left the room without a word.

Seconds later, not minutes, Dr. Eyster and this same nurse came back into the room. Both the doctor and the nurse stood in front of me, my pants down around my ankles, and stared at my knee.

After a few moments, Dr. Eyster said, "We have a really big problem here." He asked that I get up on the examining table. The nurse took off my shoes and pulled my pants off my legs. About that time, Ann entered the room. Dr. Eyster explained that I had a serious infection—serious enough that it could kill me or cause me to lose my leg. He needed to take action now. Ann and I locked eyes in shock as the doctor and nurse left the room.

Minutes later they returned with several nurses and four huge linebacker-looking guys. The nurses carried towels, while Dr. Eyster carried a scalpel and a piece of leather. He told me that he needed to get the infection out of my leg quickly, and to do that, he would have to open up my knee and express the infection. He further explained that after he was done, I would be wheeled over to the hospital, where they were waiting to remove all the screws and staples from my last operation. They would then insert an IV drip that was filled with antibiotics to try to flush the infection from my leg and knee.

While it didn't sound like a lot of fun, I understood everything—with one exception.

"So why the leather and the scalpel?" I asked.

"We have to start work right now," he said. "The leather is for you to put between your teeth so I can cut into your knee."

"No anesthesia?" I asked.

Dr. Eyster answered, "I'm sorry. We don't have any time."

Not a comforting answer.

He further explained that the big guys were to hold me down as he opened me up and expressed the nasty infection. With that, two of the guys pinned my shoulders to the table, the other two pinned my legs down, and Dr. Eyster placed the leather in my mouth. I bit down hard as he used the scalpel to open up my leg. The pain was biting, but I didn't pass out.

Ann watched the whole thing. She later said they got cups of what looked like chicken fat out of my leg. Once done, they packed my knee full of gauze and wheeled me over to the hospital for a two-hour operation. I spent the next week in the hospital with two tubes attached to my right knee: one to pump in antibiotic-infused saline, one to suck out the remaining nasty gunk.

Everything worked. I still have my leg, and I never had that knee worked on again. It works just fine, thank you very much.

It is interesting what this episode taught me, or perhaps reminded me. Even though I was recently out of my last surgery and still in intensive everyday rehab, I had begun to take things for granted. Until this episode, life had gotten better. I had started to lose the contrast between good and bad, feeling good and feeling pain. And without bad, you can't relish the good.

The swollen knee and the related infection and all the drama that surrounded them were a significant wakeup call that I needed to be grateful and never again take comfort for granted. It's amazing to me how human beings have the capacity to forget so quickly. For most experiences, forgetting is an important trait. Without it, why would a woman ever have a second child? But unfortunately with other kinds of pain, when we forget, we also forget the contrasting joy, and we become lazy and complacent. Maybe that is why some of the happiest people I know ensure they suffer just enough to feel the good when the pain stops.

It's just like riding a bike. It's great to feel the burn and pain in your muscles when you push yourself hard. It feels good when you stop. That contrast is what makes people smile after a huge effort.

You have good days and bad days on the bike—bad weather days, good weather days. Days when you feel strong, days when you feel weak. You always have to keep in mind that without the bad days, the good days are not as sweet.

This principle is illustrated in another story that perhaps those who don't ride a bike can relate to.

I have had the good fortune of working for some really great companies and of enjoying some amazing perks throughout the course of my career. I've felt great joy in the business opportunities I have had, whether that was the excitement of a new Smashburger opening, the pride that swelled within Pizza

> I find hope in the darkest of days, and focus in the brightest. I do not judge the universe.
>
> —Dalai Lama

Hut when we were official NCAA Final Four corporate sponsors, or the satisfaction with our efforts to raise money for transitional housing in Denver. I have had the very highest highs. I've had lows too.

Mostly my bad days at work were because of disappointing sales. The eight o'clock email that reported sales from the previous day often, unfortunately, defined the kind of day I was going to have.

The average job tenure of a CMO, which is what I have done for the last fifteen years, is no longer than twenty-four months and is typically closer to eighteen months. A CMO is a lot like the GM of a baseball team or the head football coach: you are only as good as your most recent game, or in the case of business, your last quarter.

In the first twenty-five years of my career, I had never been fired. I generally had been very successful in my business pursuits. But all good things must come to an end. And as I learned from my leather and scalpel experience, you can't really appreciate the good until you have experienced something less so.

One very early morning well before eight, I received a text from my boss asking that I come to his office. It was well-known that I got to the office early, so this was not an uncommon request. However, these inquiries usually were not made at this hour through a text message.

Something was up.

Sales had not been good, but we were pursuing a strategy that we knew would increase our profit despite dampening sales and traffic. We were executing this strategy, and sure enough, sales and traffic were down but profit was up. While the boss and I had some very direct conversation about the state of sales, I believed the direction we were going was the right one. We had made some significant progress in the brand and how we engaged with consumers. Our activities all had sound purpose and measureable positive results.

Even with progress, I felt something wasn't right. I had a premonition that the visit wasn't going to be a good one. As I walked into my boss's office, seated with him was the head of human resources, always the first sign of an execution.

As I sat down, I said, "I know what this must be about."

My boss, who showed no sign of emotion and who was staring somewhere beyond me said, "We are making a change. Do you have any questions?"

I asked, "Am I being fired?"

He said, "You obviously don't have any questions, so"—pointing to the head of HR—"she can take you through your severance package."

With that, he got up and left.

We went through my package. It was generous. We then left to pack my office (I was watched as I packed my things) while my boss told my folks that I was "pursuing other opportunities." Like most of these situations, there was not an opportunity to say goodbye. You work with people closely for years, and in an instant these relationships are discontinued.

So how can pain like this be good?

Just like the first lesson—it is inevitable you will fall off your bike—as a CMO, at some point you will be fired. I thought prior to the actual occurrence that I would be really mad if I ever got fired. Unfortunately, I am an ultra-competitive person, and I see everything as a win or a loss. Interestingly and fortunately, I didn't see this situation that way. I knew I had done everything in my power to be successful. The cards were just not in my favor.

After some serious soul searching, I see getting fired as a positive experience for me. I now better understand and appreciate what is most important to me in a job. I learned that there are three key elements that must be present for me to be fulfilled at work.

The first is relatively simple: I have to be busy, which in my mind translates to importance and—unfortunately a vain attribute—esteem. In the past I had complained that I hated getting so many emails. I calculated at one point that I was getting some kind of email or text every two and a half minutes. I also complained that I had meetings literally from the moment I arrived at work at seven in the morning until late into the evening. What I did not realize is how much I really liked this, how much I needed it—how much, and sadly so, it defined me.

The second element I need is the ability to build personal relationships and lead people around me. I have been told I have a big personality. This personality thrives on social interaction at the business level and demands the opportunity to develop teams and influence others.

The third thing I learned is that my soul is fed when I accomplish something of worth. This means taking business problems and challenges and finding creative, hard-fought solutions.

It took me a couple weeks to realize that I had been handed a gift. Once I realized this, I sent the following email to my boss:

Mr. Big,

   I am disappointed that our working relationship ended the way it did. But I appreciate the decisions that needed to be made. I learned a lot from you in the last twenty-six months, and I wish you, your family, and the team the best.

Trey

He responded with the following:

Trey,

   Thank you for your kind note. I hope you, Ann, and the boys are all doing well.

Firstly, I want to let you know how much I appreciated your passion and perseverance working with the brand and me. I know how tough your time here was as you tried valiantly to figure out how we could take our brand to market and drive a meaningful response. You did that a number of times, which is great credit to you. This is not an easy business, and some would say the task is not doable.

I had hoped to get a little time with you before you left the office, but for some reason that didn't work out. I too was disappointed in the way our relationship ended, and I must apologize for not helping you sufficiently to make things work. However, things weren't working, and I believe the ultimate decision was right for everyone, even if it was painful for you. I would be more than happy to get some time in the near future to at least say thank you in person and to afford you the opportunity to provide me with some feedback.

On a personal note, I thoroughly enjoyed working with you, and I too learned much (personally and professionally).

I would be delighted to provide a meaningful and positive endorsement of you and your capabilities, should a future opportunity need it.

Please pass my best regards to Ann. Take care, use the free time you have to enjoy a little of the life you have, breathe deeply, and go figure out the next adventure.

Very best wishes,

Mr. Big

I am grateful for getting fired. Really. It wasn't a happy experience, but it has been an important one. In many ways it was as startling and painful as getting my knee sliced open without anesthetic. But good has come of it. It has helped me to be much more appreciative of work. I have had a chance to take deep breaths and rid myself of poisonous infections, just like what was in my knee. I have been able to reevaluate what I want to accomplish with the rest of my work life. The time off has given me an opportunity to write this book and to fundamentally dive into the things that I believe. I have been able to uncover things that I believed but had never fully articulated. I have been able to understand what is most important in my professional life.

We need to learn to enjoy the rough days on the bike so the smooth days can be sweeter. Just think: if the world was all chip seal pavement, we wouldn't know how nice freshly laid, smooth asphalt really is.

The infection in my knee, while painful, painted another magnificent contrast between being healthy and not. After this infection episode, I recommitted my efforts to do everything I could to be healthy. The hospital, while filled with wonderful folks, was not where I wanted to be.

With the right attitude and perspective, good and bad form a righteous partnership.

Lesson 3
Never Be Content with Easy

What I have learned—painfully at times—is that my greatest discoveries have been made when I have pushed on even when instinct said, *Stop! Get off the bike!* I have learned that we should never be content with easy.

The recovery from the accident was a very long and painful process. There were many times I wanted to stop and figuratively get off the bike.

After two weeks in ICSU, I was promoted to the regular hospital, where I spent the next six weeks. During this time my rehabilitation was essentially having nurses lift me from the bed into a recliner. The first time they did this, I thought I was going to die. My body had so little tolerance for being manipulated that it really hurt. I could take it for only a few minutes before they lifted me back into the bed. Each day this process would repeat, and each day I would sit in the chair longer. Eventually I could be lifted into a wheelchair and be wheeled around.

At this point in my recovery, I had no use of my legs. I could move them, but they could not bear any weight because of my knee issues. My left arm and hand were in a cast, my body was immobilized with a brace that enveloped my core, and my right arm was a mass of bandages. All I had from a workable body part standpoint was the use of the fingers on my right hand.

The day I moved to the rehab hospital was a significant day. That was the day that I really knew I was going to get better. Physical therapists are an amazing group of people. The therapist who was assigned to me was a young guy, an athlete, who took me on as his biggest professional challenge.

Our team of therapists saw that Ken and I were competitive. We were certainly competitive with one another, but also competitive in the sense that we wanted to make each day better. Each day we were looking to create personal bests. Our team used this competitive fuel to push us farther and faster than we could have progressed on our own. It would have been easy for our team of therapists to follow the established protocols, go by the book, and take the unimaginative easy road. They didn't take the easy road. They pushed. They pushed us really hard.

Ken and I competed at everything, and our team encouraged it. We had a competition to see who could learn to walk first. It was a painful process, but we pushed each other through the agony. Now, it doesn't matter who won that competition (I think I did—I didn't have two broken legs), because in the end we were both walking again. We both won.

Once we could both walk, the competition turned to who could walk farther each day. Because of this, we gained more progress faster. We were not content with easy. There were so many times I wanted to stop because it hurt bad and I was exhausted, but I did not. I'd look over at Ken—or when Ken wasn't in sight, I'd imagine Ken working hard—and I would press on and not get off my bike.

This competition and the dedicated work of our therapists significantly helped us recover. We discovered that we could do things others thought we would never be able to do because nobody on our team was content with easy.

Because of our progress, we became the focus of the rehab hospital's advertising efforts. For a period of time, we would open the newspaper to find our pictures and a story about our recovery. This prompted one of the local TV affiliates to also cover our story. Our fifteen minutes of fame lasted less than five minutes, but ultimately it led Ken to his wife, Sandy, so it was five minutes well spent.

Our injuries were unique. The hospital had rarely encountered patients with injuries like ours who were still alive, so they had to design the recovery protocols specifically for us. I think it was actually fascinating for the doctors and therapists to find completely new ways of doing things to accommodate our injuries. When it came time for them to teach me to walk again, they had to specially design a walker for me. I could put no pressure on my left arm and very little on my right one. The walker they built looked space age, fit me perfectly, and did the job great.

The first use of the walker was less than spectacular, however. They wheeled me to one of the rehab rooms, where I was introduced to my walker for the first time. They positioned my wheelchair behind it. Four therapists surrounded me. They put a big leather belt around my waist, and one therapist positioned himself behind me with two others on my sides. The head therapist—a short blond woman who had built the walker—was in front. On a count of three, the therapists lifted me up and held me in position as the therapist in front fastened me to the walker.

Standing was a new experience for me, and new experiences in the rehab hospital usually hurt. This hurt really bad. I leaned forward to rest my face on the shoulder of the therapist. After overcoming some dizziness, we all, in sync, moved one step—my first step. It hurt. It hurt really bad. The pain drove my face farther into my handler's shoulder. With the second step, I took I bite out of her shoulder. She screamed. I screamed.

My first post-accident walk ended after two steps and a bite to the therapist's shoulder. Things got much better after that.

Not being content with easy obviously meant we had to work really hard at everything in the rehab hospital. We had three sessions each day; I worked up to about two hours in each session.

In the morning our rehabilitation was about gaining range of motion by being tortured. The physical therapist would pull and push my joints to break the scar tissue that had resulted from the accident and the surgeries. After this fun they would electrocute me with an electrical stimulator device that would remind my muscles what it was like to fire and move. More than once, either Ken or I would turn up the other's stim device and give the other a surprising jolt.

> Unfortunately we often get praise for things that weren't particularly difficult to achieve. If we focus on the props and encouragement of those who have low expectations for us, we become mediocre. It can be challenging to set our sights on excellence, particularly when we're hearing that we're already there. One of life's greatest lessons, which we all must learn, could be expressed in the phrase "That was nothing. Watch this." Challenge yourself and others to call the normal things normal and save that word excellent for things that really are.
>
> —ALEX HARRIS

Our second session was midday occupational therapy—put round blocks in round holes, that sort of wildly stimulating stuff. It was important to reteach our brains how to grasp and recognize round holes as being different from square ones. This therapy also helped us regain our tolerance for sitting and making normal body movements.

The afternoon session was filled with more physical activity, like trying to ride the stationary bike, walking around the track, and learning to walk up and down stairs and around obstacles. These were great days—selfish days. I focused only on getting better.

Several years ago, when Ann, the boys, and I were deep into living our Colorado dream, we had a number of yearly visitors who would make our house a starting place for cycling adventures through the Rocky Mountains.

These adventures always taught us important lessons and, time and again, showed us that by not stopping when we were tired or cold, we could find something new that otherwise we would have missed. We learned that you can't stop too soon or you won't discover what's around the next turn. A trip we planned through Rocky Mountain National Park, up Mount Evans, and then back to our home was no exception to this rule.

It may have been 1994, but the exact date doesn't really matter. We had an abnormally wet spring and early summer in the Rockies. Our old Wichita riding group had been planning an epic adventure starting in Loveland, Colorado, riding up to the town of Estes Park through Rocky Mountain National Park, and down through Winter Park for the first day. Day two would be easier, taking us from Winter Park up and over Berthoud Pass down to Idaho Springs. The third and final day would take us from Idaho Springs to the summit of Mount Evans (14,000-plus feet) with a finish at my house in the Ken Caryl Valley in Littleton, Colorado.

When the group gathered at my house from various out-of-state origins, it was raining—hard. When we drove to Loveland to begin the ride, it was raining—harder. When we got on our bikes in full weather gear, it continued to rain. As we climbed up along the Big Thompson River on our way to Estes Park and Rocky Mountain National Park, it got colder. As we paused at the ranger station to pay our entrance fee, we decided to press on even though it felt as if the rain was getting thicker, the temperatures colder, and our breath more visible.

As we climbed through the park, passing motorists stopped along the side of the road to look at buffalo and elk, we began to question our sanity as the thick rain turned to heavy white and abundant snowfall. As we continued our ascent up Trail Ridge Road, the snow began to stick to the ground. Trail Ridge Road is the highest continuous paved road in the States. It crosses the Continental Divide at Milner Pass (10,758 feet) and reaches a maximum elevation of 12,183 feet. At some point well above the Continental Divide, the snow became so thick on the road and covered us so abundantly that our wives, who were serving as car support, demanded that we get off our bikes and into the cars. Everyone obeyed—except Paul Kershisnik, whose wife was not among those serving as support. He kept pedaling.

Later, as Paul was continuing his solitary climb up the road with our string of cars slowly following him, a park ranger pulled up, lights flashing, and demanded to know what he was doing riding up Trail Ridge Road in an absolute whiteout. Paul's response determined his delirium: "It's not the cold that's bad; it's the temperature." We removed Paul from his bike and got him into a car to get warm.

It snowed on us the next two days.

Ignoring our instincts, we all rode through those storms as well. This trip was another confirmation that we as human beings can do hard things, and a little misery makes for better stories years later.

We can do hard things. Unfortunately, so many of us never learn that lesson because we stop short when a little discomfort gets in the way. In stopping, we rob ourselves of glorious discovery. We rob ourselves of getting stronger and building reserves to fortify us in the future when we need something to look back at and say, "I have done hard things before; I can do hard things again." If we had not pressed on, it would have been just another wet ride in the Rockies.

A year or so after the tour de snow adventure, the group was back at my house for another ride. This year we were going to ride the Triple Bypass in Colorado from Evergreen to Avon for day one. The Triple Bypass is a 120-mile ride complemented by 10,000 feet of climbing. After a rest day, day two of our epic ride would be a one-hundred-mile jaunt from Vail to Aspen over two passes, the highest of which is Independence Pass at

> Telling us to obey instinct is like telling us to obey "people." People say different things, so do instincts. Our instincts are at war ...Each instinct, if you listen to it, will claim to be gratified at the expense of the rest.
>
> —C. S. Lewis

12,095 feet. On days three and four, we would ditch our road bikes and climb onto our mountain bikes to ride from Aspen back to Vail on single-track and Forest Service roads with an overnight stay in a hut maintained by the 10th Mountain Division Hut Association.

On this trip we enjoyed glorious weather, deep-blue Colorado skies, and crisp temperatures—that is, until the afternoon of our first mountain biking day. As all those in Colorado know, afternoons in the mountains are plagued by thunderstorms. I knew this, and our plan was to get to the hut by two in the afternoon so we would miss the thunderstorm potential.

A serious wrong turn near the start of the day's ride, a spectacular over-the-handlebars crash by Craig Kasprzycki, and a serious overestimation of the terrain's difficulty on my part cost us about three hours, putting us seriously and dangerously behind schedule.

As we climbed the trail toward our destination, we could see a storm gathering behind us. As we got higher, the black clouds got closer and the rumble of the thunder got louder.

The climb was torturously slow up a severely steep fire road. Our anxiety grew as the storm crept closer. We had topped out on the fire road and were looking for the hut when the storm hit. The temperature dropped at least twenty degrees, the raindrops began to fall hard, and the lightning and thunder were simultaneous. We were in the middle of the storm at 10,000 feet, and we could not find the hut. Our hair was on end as the electricity in the storm swirled around us. We began to panic, and we rode our bikes through the trees looking for the hut while lightning struck the ground around us more than once. It was cold, and the fear was almost debilitating.

John Lauck found the hut first. He alerted us and, highly motivated, we all rode as fast as we could to the hut. We skidded to a stop, threw our bikes on the porch, and burst into the hut.

Ten habit-wearing nuns greeted us there.

We stood there, dripping wet and dumbfounded. We knew we had the possibility of sharing the hut based on our reservation, but nuns? Shivering quickly cleared our minds, and the desire to get warm overcame any other thoughts. The nuns sprung into action to provide us with blankets and soup.

The moral here, as it is in almost every situation where you press on, is that you get to experience something you would not have had the opportunity to see. This was a great experience because we pushed on even when instinct said, *Stop! Get off the bike!* Pressing on provided an experience of a lifetime: sleeping with nuns in a 10th Mountain Division Hut.

Pushing on despite obstacles is a key ingredient to business success too. I found nothing is easy in business. In fact, it is downright hard. Malcolm Knapp, a restaurant industry expert, has said, "The restaurant business is simple. Simple is hard." That can be said of many things. In almost every situation we find ourselves in, no matter how brilliant the idea may be, it won't be easy. Instinct may

Left to right–Craig Kasprzycki. Jeff Wheeler. John Lauck. and Trey Hall. This photograph was taken at the tenth mountain division hut the morning after barging in on the ten habit-wearing nuns at the height of a Colorado afternoon thunderstorm.

say the obstacles are insurmountable, but if you want to achieve them, you'll need to keep pedaling forward.

Many years ago, my friend Tom Ryan had a great burger idea. At the time he was working at McDonald's as their chief concept officer. He pitched the idea to his peers on the leadership team without much support. The idea languished at McDonald's because few other than Tom supported it.

After Tom left McDonald's to go to Quiznos as the chief concept officer, the idea again began to percolate in his head. The timing wasn't right, but the idea was nearly formed in his brain. He just needed the right opportunity.

A few years later, Rick Schaden sold half of his stake in Quiznos and created Consumer Capital Partners, a private equity company that is now serving in many ways as a new concept incubator. Rick brought Tom over from Quiznos, and the first thing Tom did was start Smashburger. That was in 2007. In 2011, *Forbes* added

Smashburger to its list of America's Most Promising Companies—privately held up-and-comers with compelling business models, strong management teams, notable customers, strategic partners, and precious investment capital.

Tom did not give up when that very quiet, negative voice that is in all our heads said, "Stop, this is too hard." The success of Smashburger is yet one more example of nothing being easy, but great success can be achieved when you ignore what's easy and press on. Don't get off your bike. Keep pedaling. Never be content with easy.

Lesson 4
Focus Keeps You Whole

One of the fundamentals that biking has taught me is the need to stay focused while riding. A wandering mind will always lead to trouble. Keeping focused keeps you whole.

As a young member of the Church of Jesus Christ of Latter-Day Saints, I served a Mormon mission. I was sent to Taiwan, the Republic of China.

In Taiwan, missionaries rode monstrously heavy, black, steel bikes. These bikes are legend throughout Taiwan, not only with the missionaries but also with the Chinese population. It was easy to identify yourself when you were walking around, not riding, as the guys who ride the "really tall bicycles." There was always an immediate acknowledgment of who we were. We rode these bikes almost everywhere and in almost all conditions. These bikes were tanks, and I had no problem riding them over curbs, rocks, or any other obstacles. In many ways these were the original cyclocross bikes. Just like in cyclocross, there were many times I had to pick up the fifty pounds of steel and jump over a *binjo,* which is Japanese for toilet. There are lots of Japanese words left over from their occupation of the island—binjo happens to

It was a bike like one of these three in the picture that I was riding in the blinding rainstorm when an old woman ran from between parked cars into our path. I was able to avoid her. but my companion was not.

be my favorite. Most streets had a binjo or open sewage system, running alongside the road. Some were bigger than others, and many times you had to jump across them to get where you wanted to go.

When something went wrong with one of these bikes, we didn't take them to anything like the high-end, pristine shops that service my stable of bikes today. Instead, we took them to a guy on the side of the road with a big hammer and some old greasy rags who, after some hammering and grunting, generally had the bike back in working order. This is obviously a significant contrast to how I maintain my bikes today.

As Mormon missionaries, we always traveled in pairs on our big, tall, black bikes. I had many companions of all shapes and sizes. With one of these partners, I learned a great lesson on focus and how a lack of it can get you into big trouble.

The following is from my Mormon missionary journal dated April 7, 1982:

Today my companion ran over an old lady in the street and broke her leg.

It was raining really hard—dogs and cats.

We were late for a discussion [a lesson that the missionaries use to teach about the Church], so we took a shortcut through the Shir Lin night market area. The roads are narrow to begin with, and with cars parked on either side of the street, it gets even narrower.

The corrugated tin roofs cast the rainwater into the middle of the street. Because it was raining so hard, it was like a whole bunch of hoses were pouring into the middle of the street—the only place we could ride our bikes.

We had our rain slickers on and our umbrellas were up. We used the umbrellas to fight off the water pouring down from the roof.

We were riding fast when all of a sudden this old woman ran from between two parked cars trying to get from the shelter of one side of the road to the other. She ran in front of me, but because of my superior athletic ability, I was able to dodge her. My companion was not so lucky. They both went down hard. My companion was out cold, face up with water pouring down into his face. I thought he might drown. The lady was moaning and screaming in the middle of the road. Instantly a crowd of angry Taiwanese gathered and pulled the old lady out of the rain and onto the sidewalk. I did the same for my companion.

The crowd all seemed to be Taiwanese. I only found one guy in the crowd who could speak Chinese; the rest were only speaking Taiwanese. [We were in a section of town that was mostly indigenous Taiwanese. These folks for the most part speak only Taiwanese, which I spoke very little of.] I asked the Chinese speaker what usually happened in a *situation like this. They said the old lady's family would be called, we should wait, and once they arrived and sized up the situation, they would tell me how much money to pay. That didn't sound too good to me, so I left my companion in the middle of the mob and went to find a phone to call the mission office, which was supposed to be staffed by other missionaries.*

Nobody was there.

As a last resort, I called the mission president [the responsible adult in charge of the 150 missionaries in a mission] instead. Now, you just don't call President Powelson unless there is a big problem. This is a big-time thing, and this was a big deal. He answered, I told him what had happened, and he told me what he thought I should do.

As we finished, the ambulance showed up, and the driver came over to speak with me. It was clear that everyone thought we were the ones at fault. The driver took me over to the ambulance as his partner put the old lady in the back and told me to get in. I told them I wouldn't get in, but I would give them my address and phone number [the mission office]. The ambulance left and we went home, wet, tired, and scared. My companion is okay. He has a headache and is soaked to the bone.

Eventually the family of the elderly lady we hit sued the church. After negotiations, some kind of settlement was reached. We visited the lady and her family several times in an attempt to apologize but never made much headway in that direction. We did learn that she fully recovered, thank goodness.

The rain pouring from the corrugated roofs and into our faces was a big distraction. It caused us to lose focus and crash. That distraction is no different than the turmoil we as bike riders and human beings face every day. These distractions can easily cause us to lose our direction. When we lose focus, many times we wobble and eventually crash—or in this case, run into an innocent old lady and break her leg.

The key is to have tools that keep you focused.

From both a business and a personal perspective, that tool for me has been the development of both brand and personal architectures.

From a business perspective, a well-conceived architecture focuses business chaos and transforms that energy into a powerful unified platform to build revenue. It is amazing to me how few companies or individuals have taken the time to put pencil to paper and truly understand who or what they are.

> The main thing is keeping the main thing the main thing.
>
> —German Proverb

Too often brands and people assume they know what their values are and, as important, what their brand essence is—really understanding what business they're in. I believe once a brand architecture is written, when distraction comes, like rain pouring down from the corrugated rooftops, we'll have enough focus to avoid the lady in the street and not crash.

I have been able to write brand architectures for a number of companies, from established, mature companies to start-ups. I have also written brand architectures and created brand books for non-profit organizations. The importance of these documents is real.

One of my bike industry heroes is Mike Sinyard, founder and CEO of Specialized Bicycles. He is a believer in brand architectures. After some significant success in the mid-1990s, Specialized turned to a group of consultants to help them plot the future of the business. This was a logical thing to do—hire really smart people to assess the business and help plot a successful future.

There was one flaw in this process, however. These consultants were not grounded in the DNA of the bike company that Mike had founded. And almost tragically, at this point Mike had not synthesized his beliefs and put them on paper. He had not written his brand book. He had not cemented his business beliefs into a Specialized bible that would keep focus on the essence of the brand when others would want to change it.

So these consultants led Mike and Specialized into a near-terminal direction by cheapening the quality of the Specialized products and selling them at mass merchandisers. Specialized lost its street credibility. Only after Mike fired the consultants and turned his attention back to his values and then—importantly—put it in a brand book was the company able to pull out of its spin and become the incredible success it is today.

The Specialized brand book is now the seminal document that leads the company's direction. It is used every day to help insulate the company from misdirection and immerse new employees in the culture of Specialized, to keep everyone one focused and spinning down the right road.

When done right, building a brand architecture is a collaborative effort that, once written, will be embraced by the organization and used on an almost daily basis. Just like at Specialized, the architecture, which has as its outcome a brand book, must be the guiderail for all business decisions. While it may seem incredibly simple, you need to literally ask yourself: is this decision consistent with the essence of the brand and with the other parts of the brand architecture? You can only know if that answer is yes by having a brand architecture.

In today's highly competitive world, it is not good enough to think you and those that you work with know what the brand stands for and what the nonnegotiable values are. Without the commitment of thinking about these standards and insights, discussing them, and finally committing them to paper, when the rainwater comes cascading down from the corrugated roof, you will be blinded, your focus will fail, and you could make poor brand choices.

With some concern that the following explanation will be too much like a textbook, I want to share a bit about the anatomy of a brand architecture. A basic architecture has several components:

Brand Fundamentals

- Brand essence, or the business you're really in, is the fundamental statement that defines what the brand is today and what the brand will be in the future. It is the core of what the brand does and how it does it.
- Brand position is that little piece of real estate in the consumer's head that only your brand owns.
- Company values are what is important and will not be compromised.
- Brand personality is the human qualities and characteristics that consumers find attractive.

Brand Strategies

- Customer identification, targeting, and segmenting require knowing who the customers are, what they want, how they spend, what they buy.
- Brand strategy is how the brand's essence is articulated within the competitive context of the current marketplace.
- Business sourcing asks who the competitors are, and how the brand wins with each of these competitors. This is an often overlooked component of brand architecture within the nonprofit world.
- Brand promise asks what highest-order benefit the brand can promise to the consumer.

- Tone of voice is the attitude that sets the brand apart from all the other brands out there.

On a company level, these issues should be covered as a group. Once all these aspects have been addressed, debated, answered, and debated some more, you need to memorialize them in a brand book. This book can be as simple as answers to the questions. This is the putting-pen-to-paper part. Ideally and most effectively, the brand architecture will be given the credit it deserves if the book itself becomes an extension of the architecture. If you are in a highly creative company and your brand architecture is articulated on an eight-and-half-by-eleven piece of paper, what credibility will the document hold, and what does that say about your company? On the other hand, what does it say to potential investors or others when you present a well-conceived articulation of your company in a format that is equally creative? It says you know what you are doing and your chances of long term success are significant. The bottom line is that the words of the architecture matter, but so does the presentation of those words.

Personal architectures are just that—personal. They should reflect your personal values, both in a real and aspirational sense. Ingredients for a personal architecture could include standards, values, activities, and other life components.

A personal architecture can help you determine your boundaries before you are faced with choices. Making important personal choices before you need to can save a lot of personal anguish. And just like a brand architecture, this personal architecture should be documented in writing and reviewed with some regularity to reinforce your personal brand in your mind.

A brand architecture should be in the hands of every organization, whether it is for-profit, nonprofit, or start-up, and even if it's a well-established brand (and of course individuals). This will ensure focus in times of distraction. A wandering mind will always get you into trouble.

Keeping focus is vitally important to avoid riding into potholes and running over old ladies.

Lesson 5

It's About the Ride, Stupid

I have learned a simple truth over the course of my life: a short ride is better than no ride. To apply this to the larger scope of life, the strength of your character is based on action, not inaction.

In Colorado my family and I lived in an amazing cycling environment, the Ken Caryl Valley, a high foothill valley above Littleton. I could leave my driveway with either my mountain bike or my road bike and enjoy breathtaking scenery and heart-pounding climbs. You were either riding uphill or downhill; there was not much flat. My anticipated day at work would dictate my ride each morning: a hard day meant lots of climbing, an easy day a more relaxed ride.

It was important that I ride each morning. It was important to my physical health, my mental health, and funny enough, my spiritual health. More times than not, in the morning I would choose my mountain bike for my ride. I could get more done and get anaerobic faster on the mountain bike than I could on my road bike. I also felt it was safer. Although I had to contend with rocks, trees, and cacti, I didn't have to worry about an inattentive driver who was concerned about making it to work on time.

There were three rides I generally chose from each morning. The rides had varying degrees of climbing and length. No matter how much or little time I had, I rode the bicycle. I had promised myself when we moved to Colorado that I would do everything in my power to have a daily Colorado experience. I stayed pretty true to that promise.

During these daily morning rides, I would contemplate the details of the day, work through issues at the office, ponder how to best work with the kids, consider my relationships, and enjoy the beauty that surrounded me. On each of my mountain bike routes, I had a place where I would stop and say my prayers for the day. There was something amazing about speaking with God in this vast cathedral.

I drove myself hard on these rides. When things weren't going as well as I would've liked, I would really smash the pedals and punish myself, thinking that if I rode harder, I could exorcise the demons and make things better. I rode daily for almost seventeen years. I rode even when it was snowing and the temperature was bitter cold, but my rides were indoors then.

I built relationships on the trails as well. I saw one woman almost every day at some point along my ride. While I did not know her and never knew her name, I knew she loved the dogs that accompanied her on her hikes. For years we would exchange "good mornings," and I would smile at the dogs running back and forth across the trail. This kind of relationship built a texture into my life that would have been missing if I had failed to ride. Even short rides got me on the trail and fostered such relationships. The only extended conversation I ever had with this lady was one morning when I saw that she was walking without one of the dogs. It had been evident to me that one of the animals was older than the other and was slowing down. When I asked her where the older dog was, I knew in my heart what the answer

80

was. The dog had passed. Even though I didn't know the dog's name, I felt her loss.

I also learned something about self-preservation on one of my morning bike rides. I was grunting up the Manor House Trail. It was a relatively short climb, only about 3.5 miles to the top from my house. The killer was the 2,300 feet of climbing that topped out at 7,855 feet. This trail was like an elevator shaft—straight up—and rocky too. The trail was initially built as a road to access some hunting cabins high above the Ken Caryl Valley in the early 1900s. The trail gets its name from the historic Manor House, which was built in 1914 by the cattle baron and newspaper publisher John Shaffer. The trail is cut through some very thick scrub oak, and as you slowly climb, you can hear all sorts of animals rustling around just out of sight. Rabbits and squirrels always seemed to be active in the brush, and on numerous occasions a deer or elk would pop out of the undergrowth and startle me.

This one particular morning, as I was nearing the last third of the ride in a particularly steep section, I heard the familiar rustling of the scrub oak ahead. I thought nothing of it, as my head was down over the handlebars and I was out of the saddle doing my best to pedal my way forward. The sound became louder, as if something rather large was making its way toward the trail through the bushes, so I looked up. As I did, about ten yards ahead of me, a rather scruffy brown bear emerged from the scrub oak. I stopped. He stopped (I assume it was a he). We stared at each other. He was as startled as I was. He took off the way he came, and I took off down the hill just as fast as the dual suspension would allow me to go.

The ride was cut short, but it was the first and last time I have seen a bear up close. Doing something, getting on my bike, allowed me to experience something not many people get to experience.

When I got out of undergrad, I needed a job. Ann was pregnant with Ryan, we were living in Dallas with my mom, and we were heading to Northwestern University for grad school in the fall. Our timing was not great. I had a job lined up in construction, but before beginning that work, I wanted to at least give working in my field a shot. I had no real leads in the Dallas marketing world except for the name of an executive who had attended NU many years prior. I gave myself one day to find a job in advertising. I searched the Yellow and White Pages for all the ad agencies I could find and then knocked on doors. I talked to some folks, but the overwhelming response was "No, thank you."

> Inaction breeds doubt and fear. Action breeds confidence and courage. If you want to conquer fear, do not sit home and think about it. Go out and get busy.
>
> —DALE CARNEGIE

I saved my last visit of the day for the Richards Group, where my connection, Brad Todd, was a principal. I went to the fifth floor of the office building where TRG was located and emerged from the elevator to be greeted by a receptionist who asked me who I was there to see. I said, "Brad Todd."

She said, "Do you have an appointment?"

I said, "No."

"Is he expecting you?"

"No."

She said, "Does he even know who you are?"

I said, "No," but quickly added, "He went to Northwestern, and I will be going there, and I was hoping he might have a minute to speak to me about his experiences."

She gave me a curious look, and then called Brad's number and began to speak to him, eyeing me the whole time. She explained what I said to her and why I was there. She hung up the phone and with some surprise said, "He'll be right out."

He came right out.

We spoke for well over an hour about what I had learned in my undergraduate studies at Brigham Young University and what I would experience at NU. It was a great talk, we enjoyed each other's company, and there was a natural connection. At the end of our time, he said he would love to hire me but had nothing in account service for me. I thanked him for his generosity and left thinking that I was going to have a great experience at NU and that Monday I would start my job in construction.

Not long after getting home, I got a call from Brad. He asked me how much money I needed to make over the summer. I told him. He asked if I would be his assistant during the summer. I said sure, and he gave me about one-third more than I would have made working construction.

I got the job that started me on my career because I did something. I got on my bike.

If you don't get on your bike, if you don't knock and take action, if you don't ask for what you want, the door will never be opened and the answer can never be yes. Always knock. Always ask. Always get on the bike and take the ride. When you do, amazing things can happen.

It's about the ride, stupid.

Lesson 6
Celebrate the Pain

I am the definition of an amateur cyclist: old and slow with a stable of really nice bikes. As an amateur, I ride because I enjoy how it makes me feel. I love the knowledge that I can do hard things. When I am on the bike, unlike when I am in other situations, I can inflict my own pain and afterward celebrate it.

In many ways this opportunity to celebrate the pain is one of the greatest gifts of cycling. I have learned that during even the most difficult rides, you have to keep smiling, even laughing a bit at the pain, and then—and this I think is the most important thing—celebrate your survival.

Prior to the Salt Lake City Olympics, Coca-Cola sponsored a worldwide torch relay. The Olympic flame is a symbol of the Olympic Games—most people know this. What I did not know is that the flame itself commemorates Prometheus's theft of fire from the god Zeus, whose origins lie in ancient Greece, where a fire was kept burning throughout the celebration of the ancient Olympics. The Olympic flame was reintroduced at the 1928 Summer Olympics in Amsterdam. The torch relay of modern times was introduced at the controversial 1936 Berlin Olympics, and both have been part of the modern Olympic Games ever since.

As most people know, the Olympic torch today is ignited several months before the opening ceremony of the Olympic Games at the site of the ancient Olympics in Olympia, Greece. What most people don't know is that eleven women, representing the ancient priestesses, perform a ceremony in which the torch is kindled by the light of the sun, its rays concentrated by a parabolic mirror. I always felt that the Olympics were magical, even bordering on mystical. I now know why—eleven priestesses.

The American portion of the 2002 Olympic relay was a massive affair with segments in every state. It wound its way around the country, ending in Salt Lake City with the final few legs inside the Olympic Stadium leading up to the dramatic lighting of the Olympic cauldron, which stayed lit during the length of the games.

The SLC Olympics was the first time that I can remember that the torch relay became a big deal. In a really cool promotion, Coca-Cola provided people the opportunity to participate in the torch run by sending in stories of overcoming hardship or doing great works.

At the time of these Olympics, I was the CMO at Boston Market. We served Coke. When Ann found out about the relay, she got in touch with our Coke representative, who knew my story about the bike accident, and got things rolling. Evidently, the story was fairly compelling because they selected me to be a participant. I am sure it didn't hurt that I was the CMO of a Coke-pouring customer.

At that time, Boston Market was part of the McDonald's Corporation (the largest Coca-Cola customer in the world), so they invited the entire corporate family to come to the home of McDonald's in Chicago to run the torch and participate in all the festivities that surrounded the torch in that very big city. They had a number of key McDonald's executives running in the relay as well. Ann, the boys, and I had a great time attending some fairly elaborate parties, mingling with celebrities, and being treated like celebrities ourselves.

My part of the relay was to be run in the small town of Kenilworth. When Ann and I were in grad school at Northwestern, we dreamed of living in Kenilworth in someone's gatehouse or servants' coach house. Kenilworth has a very traditional, small downtown area, and my portion of the relay was to be run in the heart of downtown. The morning that I was to run, Ann dropped me off at the staging area, where I met with the relay officials and other runners. As we waited, the runners were all asked to tell their stories of why they were there to run the torch. Heroes—folks who had saved people from burning buildings, individuals who helped the homeless, veterans who had been wounded serving our country—surrounded me.

Then there was me, who was there because I fell off my bike.

We told our stories on the bus as we were shuttled to where we would be running. As we drove, the excitement and anticipation of running with the torch grew. Through the bus windows, we could see thousands of people gathering to watch the torch pass. There were men, women, and children, many carrying small American flags. It was heartwarmingly patriotic, something out of a movie, so surreal, and I was right in the middle of it. Even in the bus, you could feel the energy and excitement of the people who lined the streets awaiting a fleeting glimpse of the Olympic torch. It was extraordinary and humbling to be a part of this event.

The realization of just how extraordinary it really was grew for me as we dropped off runners at their designated spots along the relay route. With each departure it was closer to my turn. The feeling of anticipation and nervousness was a lot like the start of a bicycle race. I had a dry throat and a knot that started in my stomach and ended just below my Adam's apple. The kind of knot that makes you want to throw up but only allows for a little painful dry heaving. I had the uneasy sensation in my stomach and the tightness in my throat for at least thirty minutes.

The bus ride and the departures of the runners were all well orchestrated. The bus traveled about a mile ahead of the runner. Finally it was my time to get out of the bus in the center of downtown Kenilworth. The feeling of being in the middle of something so much bigger than anything I could have imagined only magnified as I got off the bus.

As I stepped off, I was escorted to the middle of the street. My appearance served to create an even greater frenzy among those lining the street. They were bundled against the cold, and their attention was divided between staring at me and gazing down the route for their first glimpse of the torch. There were literally thousands of people crowding the sidewalks of Kenilworth's main street.

While standing and waiting for the torch, I was surrounded by handlers and security. The last time I had enjoyed this much attention was in the emergency room after the accident. This was much better.

As a torch runner, I was decked out in a cool white jogging suit, an SLC Olympics hat, Olympic gloves, and some brand new running shoes. My handlers wore a similar suit, but in blue. After getting some last-minute instructions, like which way to run, how to hold the torch to be lit, how fast to run, stuff like that, I was handed my unlit torch. In the relay, it is the flame that is passed, not the torch. Who knew?

Not long after these final instructions, my handlers left me alone as a swell of cheers began just out of sight. This chorus grew as you might imagine the wave in a sports stadium might sound, if it had sound. This magic, the phenomenal energy that the sound created, grew closer as the runners ahead of me ran in my direction.

Finally I caught a glimpse of the runner just before me. As I did, so did all those waiting along the street, and a deafening cheer emanated from the masses. It was a joyous, almost spiritual sound. It got louder as the runner approached then quieted ever so slightly as the runner stopped in front of me.

For a brief moment, the flame's journey to Salt Lake City, Utah, paused as I lowered my torch toward hers and she likewise lowered the Olympic flame toward mine.

An eruption of cheers was ignited as the flame leapt to my

Trey Hall running the Kenilworth stage Olympic Torch run prior to the 2002 Salt Lake City Winter Games.

torch—the Olympic flame had been passed to me. At that moment, and for the next quarter mile, I was the only one in the world that had possession of the Olympic flame. Wow. I clutched the torch in two hands (it would be a terrible thing to drop the torch) and started down the street.

I was a rock star as I jogged down the street. My handlers in the blue suits followed me, as did "security" —a buff dude who carried a gun. As we ran, people cheered, people screamed. I ran. Before I knew it, I was lighting the next runner's torch. My flame was extinguished. My moment was over.

My moment was over, but this was far bigger than a moment. It was recognition. A powerful recognition. I was able to celebrate my pain.

Running with the torch was an amazing recognition for me and my family and friends who had battled so valiantly to get me to the point where I could actually run.

Recognition is important for everyone, at home and at work. Over the last twenty-five years, I have found it doesn't take much to help someone feel appreciated and celebrated. Asking about a child's band or athletic performance or informally recognizing a job well done in front of the team all provide the appreciation and stimulation that recognition provides. Work is a four-letter word, and no matter how much we enjoy what we do, we will feel some pain during the course of our lives and professional careers. As a friend or a business leader, we must recognize and celebrate those around us so they know how important they are to us.

> The more you praise and celebrate your life, the more there is in life to celebrate.
>
> —OPRAH WINFREY

Nearly every organization I have worked in has held formal company-wide recognitions or celebrations, some more effective than others.

I think the recognition of most impact, something I have tried to emulate, was at Pizza Hut. Steve Reinemund, now the dean of the Wake Forest Business School and recently the CEO of PepsiCo, would present people at all levels of the organization a watch that he pulled off his wrist. It wasn't like he had a wrist full of watches. Those being recognized and celebrated in front of their peers were getting the CEO's watch directly off his wrist. These were powerful moments of recognition that uplifted everyone's spirits. These were not formal moments or rehearsed speeches but rather genuine and heartfelt displays of recognition, celebration, and appreciation. These watches were treasured keepsakes for all those who received them.

In college I took a psychology class. I think everyone had to. I don't recall doing that well, but one of the lessons I do recall is the classic Maslow's hierarchy of needs. In this hierarchy, two of the

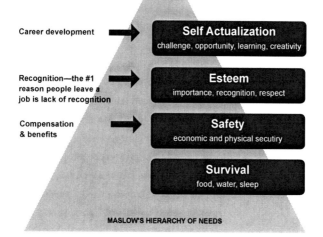

The importance of recognition

Career development → **Self Actualization**
challenge, opportunity, learning, creativity

Recognition—the #1 reason people leave a job is lack of recognition → **Esteem**
importance, recognition, respect

Compensation & benefits → **Safety**
economic and physical secutiry

Survival
food, water, sleep

MASLOW'S HIERARCHY OF NEEDS

most valuable psychological needs we have as human beings are the need to be appreciated and the need to belong. These needs are met through thanks and recognition.

As you look at the diagram, you can see how compensation and benefits support a fundamental need, but most importantly how recognition supports our higher-level psychological needs.

Remember that the purpose of recognition is to drive greater levels of discretionary effort. If recognition can reduce unwanted turnover in business, just imagine what this same principle can do at home. Such discretionary effort comes when we, as people, feel inspired to do more.

In fact, that's the whole reason I wrote this book, and it's the underlying support for the title *Pedal Forward*. As I mentioned at the beginning of this book, I sincerely believe that human beings have an amazing soul that is tougher than we think, is more compassionate than we believe, and whose true north points toward goodness and joy. As human beings in a world that will knock us off our bikes, we must be resolute in getting back on, no matter how many times we get knocked off. And once we do get back on and continue the ride, we must take time to celebrate. When we do, and when we offer to celebrate others and recognize them for their accomplishments both big and small, we begin to fulfill our measure and magnify our place on this earth.

While in the rehabilitation hospital, Ken and I continued to progress and get better. We graduated from full-time twenty-four-hour care and therapy and finally, after three months, got out of the hospital. Upon our release, our friends threw us parties at our homes. It was an important celebration for everyone involved. These parties gave all our family and friends a chance to celebrate their part in our healing process. It was a time for people to gather and laugh. We were surrounded by lots of love and support.

Recognition, in many ways, is like the Olympic torch kindled with the light of the sun by eleven priestesses. When we recognize someone, we built their fire, their Olympic torch. And as we do, this fire is passed on, much like the torch—creating a more selfless environment.

Lesson 7
Communication Helps Avoid the Potholes

Potholes, gravel, and uneven surfaces are the bane of a cyclist. These obstacles cause accidents—and sometimes death. As a result cyclists have created a language that, when properly used, can reduce the potential of riding your bike into a pothole.

In all aspects of our lives, communicating is one of the fundamental keys to success. If you know something, it's important tell it and tell it with conviction and clarity.

In the 2012 LoToJa (a sanctioned two-hundred-plus-mile race from Logan, Utah, to Jackson Hole, Wyoming), a cyclist died after crashing his bicycle and falling into the Snake River in Wyoming. The rider was approximately eight miles south of Jackson Hole on Highway 89 when he crossed a bridge over the Snake River and came upon a hazard in the roadway, believed to be a pothole, according to a press release by Sheriff Jim Whalen with Teton County:

> "[The rider] swerved to miss the hazard, over-corrected, lost control of the bicycle, and crashed into the guardrail," Whalen said. He catapulted over the guardrail and fell approximately 35 feet into the river, in water about a foot deep.

According to reports from the scene, other racers stopped and rendered aid until medical personnel arrived, but unfortunately and tragically the rider was pronounced dead at St. John's Hospital in Jackson. Coroner Kiley Campbell said the examination revealed the cyclist had suffered a cervical fracture.

Here's where communication failed: local residents had complained about the poor roads in that stretch of the race for years and shared further concern about a guardrail that was reportedly two feet high. People had been talking, but was any communication happening?

After the accident the LoToJa communications director stated, "We are questioning [the potholes], there is some rough ground [there]."

Communication is serious business. Had there been more of it in the 2012 LoToJa, either between cyclists or the LoToJa officials, concerning a notoriously rough patch of asphalt, a tragedy may have been avoided.

As Communications 101 students learn, communication is in the receiver. It is one of the few lessons I remember from college but often forget to apply. Even though our lips might be moving and our arms flailing, unless the person we are speaking to clearly understands what we mean, no communication is taking place.

> The single biggest problem in communication is the illusion that it has taken place.
>
> —GEORGE BERNARD SHAW

When I seriously started riding my bike with a group, this truth was reinforced. In my first group ride, I learned lots of new words. People were talking to me, but I had no clue what they meant.

"Car up!"

What? I look up. I ride into a pothole. There was no communication. I later learned that *car up* means "a car is coming our way." Little good it did for me then. Since then I have learned the meaning of other important cycling words:

Auger: To involuntarily take samples of the local geology, usually with one's face, during a crash.

Blow up: *See* bonk.

Bonk: To exercise to the point of depletion of the body's energy stores, leaving one extremely weak and giddy.

Cranial disharmony: How one's head feels after augering. "When my lid nailed that rock, I had a definite feeling of cranial disharmony."

Digger: A face plant. "Look at that guy on that gnarly single track. He's going to go over the bars and do a digger."

Endo: The maneuver of flying unexpectedly over the handlebars, thus being forcibly ejected from the bike. Short for "end over end."

Mantrap: A hole covered with autumn leaves, resembling solid earth—effective at eating the front wheel of the unsuspecting rider.

Road rash: Abraded skin caused by a crash.

Over-the-bar blood donor: A rider who is injured while doing an endo.

Wash out: To have the front tire lose traction, especially while going around a corner or when inadvertently locked. Generally results in the wheel ending up somewhere other than under the rider.

Painfully, I have learned that communication can be impacted by environment. I enrolled my wife in my own cycling school one summer to kill time while our sons attended a summer camp in Utah. Ann had stopped running because of knee issues and wanted to ride with me. So the Trey Hall School of Cycling was born. The school did not last long, and our marriage survived only because we have a great relationship that is built on stronger principles than cycling.

I was a poor professor and an even worse communicator. I was long on talk and short on patience. I felt the best way to share my cycling lessons with my wife was while we were riding. I did not realize this caused some environmental issues that caused a lack of communication to take place. I didn't fully appreciate that my own now-fluent cycling jargon might be a little intimidating, nor did I realize that she might have trouble hearing my instructions. She had not yet developed confidence to ride very close to me, so I had to shout my directions, which made me sound angry.

An obstacle to communication? You bet.

Further, wind and traffic noise carried many of my instructions from my mouth to someplace other than her ears. On several occasions I was convinced I had explained things thoroughly only to witness Ann completely ignore what I had just instructed or do something in the opposite way I had described it. In a husband-and-wife relationship, you might guess how I took this: *Clearly she doesn't want to learn and is ignoring my fine instruction,* I concluded.

The reality was that she heard only half of what I was saying and was doing her best to follow my instructions. She too had become frustrated when I did not answer her questions, and she believed I was ignoring her. That same external noise that drowned out my explanations caused me to miss Ann's communication. Communication occurs only when it is received—exactly what they taught us in that Communications 101 class.

In our lives off the bike, whether at home with our families or in our businesses, we need to make sure that our communication:

1. Is free of external interferences that may cause the message not to arrive. Don't try to teach while riding your bike. It's best to find a place free from distractions.

2. Has a purpose. Appropriate purpose creates interest. Without interest, no one listens. While the Trey Hall School of Cycling had a purpose, the communication I created was not specific for my pupil.

3. Is simple. There's no need to demonstrate how smart you are. The professor in this instance didn't tailor the message to the student. Instead, he tried to show how cycle-savvy he was and lost an opportunity for effective and fun interaction with his spouse.

Ann and I laugh about this experience today, but back when we were experiencing the communication breakdown, it was serious business. Communication, both giving and receiving, is a lost art, and too many people are riding into potholes because they lack the proper command of it.

Effective communication builds trust and confidence with those you ride and work with. Those who communicate in a timely and simple manner, free from other distractions, find themselves as leaders with willing followers. People have an innate need for knowing what is going on. When was the last time you were on an airplane, sitting on the tarmac for hours with no explanation? Trust and confidence—not so much. A simple update, even if it's bad news and won't change the fact that you're stuck in an immobile plane, provides a degree of humanity that everyone deserves.

Effective communication is key on a group ride, when trust and confidence are really needed. Simple, purposeful, distraction-free communication maximizes a team's effectiveness by providing team alignment. Just as both wheels of your bike should have a clear idea on where they are going, so should all members of a group. Can you imagine the disaster if the two wheels on a bike got a different message?

I was riding with a large group recently. I had fallen back to the middle of the pack after having been scolded that I was pushing the pace too hard and that I was "not in the Tour de France." I actually knew that I wasn't in France. So I fell back and watched the "leader" take the tempo (which really wasn't any slower than I was riding). He was gesturing to the guy next to him in a very animated way when he suddenly made a hard right turn onto a new road. This abrupt change caught everyone by surprise—wheels crossed, riders biffed into the pavement, and chaos ensued. Our leader had failed to communicate. We could not read his mind. We lost confidence in him. In fact, my buddy Carl and I peeled off from the group because I didn't want this bozo adding more risk to my ride. He lost my trust in a heartbeat. I never rode with that group again.

Through the course of my career, I've seen failure when people abdicate their responsibility for communication or simply take it for granted. And while leaders are the ones who need to set and model communication standards, it is not just the leaders who should follow them. Everyone must be responsible for communication and ensuring that it takes place.

When Ken and I moved from the SICU to the regular hospital, we were roommates. I had the bed closest to the door, and he had the more scenic window space. As you can imagine, we had a long list of medications that we received on a scheduled basis. It was crucial that we get the right meds at the right time to keep our healing on schedule. Proper attention and communication was at the heart of this schedule. About two weeks into our stay, there was a communication mishap. While it did not cause any major damage, it did lead to a review of the communication steps that were being employed in support of our care.

One evening as Ken and I were watching TV after a long day of healing, a nurse arrived at my bedside with two pills in a little white cup. Her arrival seemed very natural. I'm sure Ken and I were consumed with the TV when she handed me the cup and a glass of water. Instinctively, I downed the pills and went back to watching the TV program. Not too long after consuming the two pills, I began to have an out-of-body experience and began to sing, badly, "Tiny Bubbles" by the late Hawaiian singer Don Ho. I'm sure Ken was amused by my singing, but he was also concerned with his own increasing pain. Not long after I started singing, Ken pushed the call button and nicely asked when he might be receiving his pain medication. The nurse reminded him that she had just been there to administer his medication. He would just have to wait. He assured her that wasn't the case. There was a pause on the phone, followed by a muffled comment and a "We'll be right there."

Clearly I had received Ken's pain meds on top of my own, which got me high enough to remember the words to "Tiny Bubbles" and uninhibited enough to sing them loudly.

Ken finally did receive his medication, but unfortunately I continued to sing for a bit longer. This lack of communication, the lack of clarity, drove this situation into a pothole. Communication, like this example illustrates, requires active participation, not casual observance.

Effective communication also requires curiosity. What I have found is that you need to ask questions to be a good communicator and receive the most out of any interaction. It again goes back to the point that communication is an active sport, not a passive one. Key questions for enhanced communication in business or your personal life are:

- What you need (information or action—remember purpose)
- What to ask
- Who to ask
- What to tell the person (to bring them up to speed) so that he or she can give you the best action you need

While it might be a revelation to some, communication requires intelligence. Several years ago when Ann and I were living in Denver, I had the responsibility at our church for teaching young men ages sixteen to eighteen. This was an interesting group. Of the ten or so in the group, all but about two would be considered jocks.

Two things motivated these kids: sports and girls. It was clear to me that although they were decent high school athletes, they would not be earning their college tuition by playing sports. It was also clear to me, from years of experience, that their jock mentality would not translate to long-term success with the ladies, or with life in general.

So I started an it's-not-cool-to-be-stupid campaign during our time together. In our meetings I required real answers to questions—not answers an elementary school student would offer.

"I don't know" answers were not accepted and were aggressively persecuted. With all my might, I tried to instill in these young men that to be respected, to be counted as someone to be trusted with a job or a girlfriend, thoughtful, carefully crafted communication needed to come out of their mouths. Slowly the lessons took hold and eventually they began to police themselves. More than a few times, the kids would say, "It's not cool to be stupid," to one of their peers.

Sadly, many people in the business world have not yet learned this lesson. Either we are not teaching simple communication skills in school or people have become lazy, or they don't care. Some of the communication I've received over the course of my career has been almost criminal. When I receive correspondence that is addressed to someone else, is punctuated poorly, has misspellings, or is just plain sloppy, I immediately throw the offending piece away or delete it from my computer. Why would I do business with someone who has so little regard for communicating? I can believe only that they would apply the same disregard to my business.

It's not cool to be stupid. It's so not cool, you won't get my business.

Finally, as we communicate, we must understand how people process communications in our fast-changing world. For the most part, people no longer read long paragraphs or long sentences, and they have no patience for long emails or text messages. We live in a 140-digit Twitter world. You have to be interesting, simple, brief, yet brilliant.

As Jim Rohn mentions, take every opportunity to exercise communication, to be the best at it you can be so that you can rise to your potential and help others steer away from potholes.

> Take advantage of every opportunity to practice your communication skills so that when important occasions arise, you will have the gift, the style, the sharpness, the clarity, and the emotions to affect other people.
>
> —JIM ROHN

Lesson 8
There Is Importance in the Peloton

Who you ride with and how they behave is a reflection of you, so you must carefully choose who you ride with. There is importance in your peloton. This is one of the fundamental truths that I have learned over time: for better or worse, people are counted with those whom they stand next to. As a result we should obviously try to stand next to the best and brightest. And when behavior is not what it should be, we must take immediate corrective action. This may mean leaving a company so your reputation is not tarnished.

I have had the privilege of working with some of the best human beings on the planet. I have also unfortunately associated with some unsavory characters. The difference in the way you feel about yourself and the work you do when you're involved with good humans is profound.

Pizza Hut in the nineties was filled with the brightest minds and the most compassionate hearts in the restaurant world. One story that I am fond of remembering concerning good humans occurred in the first few days after the accident. Steve Reinemund, the Pizza Hut CEO, was at the hospital holding vigil with many of our other coworkers. Pause a moment and consider that sentence: a CEO holding a vigil at the hospital with the rank and file for the rank and file. Steve's presence was a powerful message for the Pizza Hut community. By his action he was demonstrating that everyone stood together at Pizza Hut. Everyone clearly saw Steve was someone they wanted to ride with.

During the course of hanging around the waiting room on this particular day, Steve was introduced to my mother. They began to talk, and Steve asked where she lived. Upon hearing she was from Dallas, he asked how she got to Wichita. My mom mentioned that she had driven. Steve expressed his concern that she had made the long trip by herself. My mom explained she had no other choice. Steve then declared that while I was recovering, anytime she needed to come and visit, she was to call him and he would make arrangements for her. That kind of offer doesn't happen often.

This was an example of the great company that Pizza Hut was at that time, led by great, compassionate, human executives.

Our pay further exemplified this compassion. The entire time Ken and I were out of work, we were never placed on disability, which would have reduced our paycheck substantially. Pizza Hut kept us on full pay for the entire time we were gone. There was never any worry that I can remember that I would not have a job when I returned. I'm sure in some degree this helped us both recover quickly.

All of this may be a very nice story, but what I believe makes it a great story is that Pizza Hut was not only a place where there was humanity, but it was also an organization that demanded excellence. Our CEO drove this expectation. Nothing but the best would do for Steve. He expected and got the best from everyone. While Pizza Hut was not void of business politics, it was the least political place I have ever worked. Steve held people accountable (he was tough—Naval Academy tough), but he also encouraged his folks to reach and stretch, and with that, to make some mistakes.

Let me illustrate this point. While this is not a bike story, it does involve a fine man I rode my bike with, John Lauck, now CEO of the nonprofit Children's Miracle Network. John was a VP of marketing at Pizza Hut with specific responsibility over events and movie tie-ins. We had signed a deal with the producers of *Back to the Future II* starring Michael J. Fox. We'd had a series of great successes with movie tie-ins, most notably *The Land before Time,* where we sold hand puppet characters from the movie for $1.99 with a pizza purchase. With this success in hand, John set out to create a strong tie to the movie with an added-value premium to be sold at Pizza Hut. He worked with the movie's creative team and producers, and solar shades were born. Solar shades were funky sunglasses that the characters in the movie would wear. The strategy was that because the characters would be sporting the glasses, they would become a fashion rage, and millions of fashionistas would flock to Pizza Hut, buy a pizza, and for just $1.99 be involved in the next fashion craze.

It was a great plan. Unfortunately, the scenes where the funky solar shades were worn in the movie ended up on the cutting room floor. What we ended up having was a bunch of ugly sunglasses and no real tie to the movie—a flop. We didn't sell many sunglasses, nor did we sell much pizza.

John was responsible. I don't recall him blaming the studio or anyone else for the poor performance. He took complete accountability in some very tough meetings. He recalls strongly believing that he would be fired because of the failure. When he saw Steve walking down the hall to his office near the end of the crisis, he believed his time had come.

Steve walked to his door, knocked, asked to come in, shut the door, and sat down. The discussion wasn't about being fired; it was a meeting acknowledging John's accountability, that he should learn from the failure, and that he should move on.

In the end, solar shades were sold in some third-world country for pennies on the dollar.

Unfortunately for many, those days of straightforward accountability and responsibility are over. In many cases we are now embraced

> Individual commitment to a group effort—that is what makes a team work, a company work, a society work, a civilization work.
>
> —VINCE LOMBARDI

by new personal strategies that create distance from problems, shed blame, and no longer foster the personal yet accountable paths of the past. I call these issues the economy of deflection. This economy of deflection is unfortunately pervasive not only in business but also in personal relationships. At some time or another, you have experienced the currency of this negative trend, which includes:

- The slow no
- Forming a committee
- The "I didn't know" syndrome
- The pocket veto

We'll explore all these soon, but in short, you don't want to put this currency in your business or personal bank. You want to ride with those who give you their best, not with those who withhold their best from you. Can you imagine riding with a group, getting a flat, not having a tube, and one of your riding buddies not sharing his spare with you?

Unfortunately, so many in people today are withholding their spare tubes, not sharing with their all, and actually thwarting progress because of their deflective selfishness. These behaviors are negatively influencing how companies and just plain ol' people deal with complexity, bureaucracy, and decision making today, individually and collectively creating frustration.

In order to be all we can be, in order to create the best peloton, we need to ride away from these behaviors. If you see these behaviors in your organizations or within yourself, get rid of them. When you do, you can significantly improve productivity and progress, so you can become the person you were intended to be.

On the following pages, you'll find the currency of deflection that I find most heinous.

The Slow No

The slow no is an escape for cowards. In the economy of deflection, it is used when a leader, employee, or acquaintance does not have the wherewithal (read: guts) to say no when the answer is clearly no. This deception creates waste—waste of time and waste of human dignity.

In our degenerative workplace environments, this currency is used with the hope that by not saying anything, by not being accountable for delivering the uncomfortable no, the problem or decision will just go away, or better yet someone else will take accountability and take the tough step to tell the truth.

The slow no costs people money, which makes it even more criminal. If this tactic is employed within an organization, it wastes precious energy on projects that should not have begun in the first place or should have been shut down much sooner. Externally the slow no costs vendors time and energy by pursuing activities that the client has no intention of executing.

Let me share a real-life and recent example of this. My wife and I will retire to a beautiful mountain home. Near our place of retirement is a fast-growing four-year university. I began a correspondence with them in an effort to get to know the faculty and size up the opportunity of one day potentially teaching on an adjunct basis there. I told them I would fly up on my own dime, meet with them, and speak to their students on the topic of their choice. What transpired was typical of the slow no. It appears to me they didn't want to say yes but couldn't find the guts to say no. So they led me on with just enough communication to satisfy their guilt and feed my hope that this would work out.

Did they want to avoid hurting my feelings?

Being told no up front would have been far better than engaging in a four-month ordeal of offering to spend my money for their benefit but acquiring only a string of unanswered emails and some personal resentment.

Would it have been easier to say they were not interested up front? Yes. Should I have given it up earlier? Yes. Unfortunately I dug in, hoping that it would work out. In many ways I am as guilty as they are. I should have recognized the slow no earlier, been stronger, and moved on sooner.

Forming a Committee

The second cousin to the slow no is the formation of a committee. Realistically, how often do we stare an issue in the eye (or allow others to do so) and then declare we need to call a meeting, organize a cross-functional group, demand more data, and set up a committee, all to avoid taking responsibility for making a much-needed decision? Low confidence, fear, and laziness all contribute to this form of avoidance. But avoiding accountability and responsibility has no value other than as a key currency in the economy of deflection.

In business and in life, we must become comfortable with the notion of making decisions, doing so in a timely and informed way, and holding ourselves and others accountable for the consequences of those decisions. In many cases, the right decision is the one that causes us to be most uncomfortable (like saying no to a colleague—see the slow no?). To be successful, we have to learn to live with the discomfort for a while. Rest assured, it goes away when the right result is forthcoming!

Being decisive is a requirement of life. Making a decision and living with the consequences glorifies our progress. Making decisions is where we make a difference and where we add value as human beings. Delegating a decision up or down should simply be a function of who is best equipped to make the decision and not meant as a delaying or avoidance tactic. Making decisions on the basis of good information and balancing risk is a necessity, but organizing bureaucracy to deflect the decision from you or defer the decision to others is always a bad thing. Group input is always good, but group decision making (committees and the like) rarely tends to be efficient or smart when tough decisions need to be made.

The "I Didn't Know" Syndrome

Claiming no knowledge of things we should know about or declaring we have been "asking that question for forever" is another cowardly and dishonest currency in the economy of deflection.

About the turn of the century (2000, not 1900) I started hearing "I don't know about this" as a deflection technique. As bad as "I don't know about this" is, the "I've been asking about this for months (or since I arrived)" statement may be worse. What message does this send to those around us? If you consider that universally our jobs, whether they're at home or in the office, aren't to simply ask questions—they're to get answers and then do something with the information—we see that this excuse shows simply that we're failing. We should be informed about our businesses or other affairs.

Staying current, asking pertinent questions, being resourceful, and following through until answers are received are our obligation. It's the way we grow and become who we are destined to be. Our lifelong job is to seek learning and to develop wisdom. We fail when we say, "I didn't know," when in fact we should have known.

Those who utter "I didn't know" lack honesty, integrity, and work ethic. "I didn't know" is not the statement of a leader. It should not be the statement for anyone in business. These words lead to contempt and resentment from others, resulting in unproductive and damaging relationships. In the work environment, these statements do not inspire confidence, as employees must question, "Why don't our executives know what's going on?" or, worse still, "Why do they say they don't know when they do?"

The Pocket Veto

The pocket veto refers to the passive-aggressive behavior of ignoring what has been agreed to without providing challenge or an indication that something will *not* get done. The easiest way for any of us to avoid conflict is to passively agree or implicitly suggest we will comply by not resisting and then to ignore the agreement. On the surface it seems that ignoring the task is less painful than challenging it in the first place. In a world where accountability is lower than it should be and performance management is not the norm, the pocket veto can be exercised with gay abandon. Plans will fail to be executed and expectations will not be met.

Gossip, innuendo, and off-the-record conversations are the toolkit of passive-aggressive behavior and the pocket veto. If a leader sidesteps the direct delivery of bad news and instead feeds this indirectly through others, he deflects the responsibility of communicating meaningfully and directly with peers and subordinates. He devolves to passive aggressiveness. This currency undermines the company's integrity and saps confidence and trust from those around him.

So what really allows the pocket veto to thrive as a currency of deflection is a lack of alignment and relevance, and almost certainly the lack of a clear purpose with weak-kneed members in your peloton.

In some instances, the lack of suitable consequences can also cause the pocket veto to be exercised. The antidote therefore is not an increase in accountability, but instead, gaining alignment and creating relevance, all cemented through a very clear purpose for what needs to be done.

A warning here: gaining alignment is not the same thing as gaining consensus! A consensus is something we can all subscribe to and agree to. Alignment means everyone understanding something the same way and clearly seeing the relevance, but it doesn't always entail agreement. Not everything we do or say will involve agreement or consensus, and that's okay. Sometimes the best we can do is align. It's like a group ride when everyone does not agree on what the route will be. But in the end, everyone is on their bikes and heading in the same direction.

I have been very lucky, or perhaps I have chosen well, to ride with a strong group. Those I ride with have made me stronger, have called me out when I have strayed into the currency of deflection, and helped me change my ride. As I mentioned at the beginning of this chapter, who you ride with and how they behave is a reflection of you. You must choose carefully. There is importance in your peloton, because in the end we will be counted among those whom we ride with, those whose reputations when mingled with ours form an impression. I believe we all want to be counted among those who gave their all. We want to be associated with wonderful people versus those who rode really fast but lost respect because they tainted themselves with their own and others' disgrace.

Lesson 9
Always Know Your Map

Bike riding, like life, requires we practice persistence and acknowledge that it's always okay to change where you go, but it's not okay to change your values. You need to know your personal map—your values—and persistently stick to them.

After I ran the Olympic torch in 2002, it was time to come home. Post-9/11 airport security was a new and difficult experience for travelers. Faced with this new security hurdle and carrying an odd object such as the torch, I was a bit concerned.

Prior to even traveling to Chicago to run with the torch, I had called O'Hare airport security. This was 2002—the Transportation Security Administration (TSA) was not yet in place, so was security was handled by private contractors at each airport. I told them about my pending travel and what would be accompanying me home from Chicago. Upon reaching someone who sounded like she had some authority, I was told that it would be fine—"No problem," she said. I felt better but still wasn't convinced that it would be that easy. So the morning of our departure, I called the airport one more time and was once again told that there should be no problem. I felt a little better but wanted one last assurance, so I called someone I had met the day before who was also taking a torch home through O'Hare and was leaving on an earlier flight. This guy said he had been through security with no issue and was getting on his flight. I felt better—I'd had three confirmations that it was a go with the torch.

The torch was a big hit everywhere Ann, the boys, and I went. From the rental car return to the airport ticket counter, people approached us and asked to hold the torch and have their picture taken with it. We were happy to oblige. As we moved from place to place, Dallin, who was twelve years old at the time, was designated to carry the torch. He was the most responsible of the boys and the least likely to drop it.

Despite the assurances that security would not be a problem for us, to say I wasn't apprehensive as we came to the security area would be untrue. As we stood in line for the conveyor belt to take all carry-ons through the x-ray machines, the nausea that I had experienced just prior to running the torch returned.

Once it was our turn, we put all our stuff on the x-ray conveyor belt. I placed the torch on top of our coats and watched as it disappeared into the boxy x-ray machine. My heart was pounding, and my stomach was in my throat, tempting my gag reflex. I knew I wasn't doing anything bad, but I'd had a constant premonition of impending doom. Trying not to show I felt this way, I put on a smile and walked through the security gate, keeping an eye on the belt. If it stopped and the guy leaned into his screen, that would indicate he was concerned about something. The belt stopped, and the guy leaned into the screen to look at my torch.

As I watched him inspect the image of my torch, my heart raced even faster, and my nausea threatened to become a real problem.

The x-ray monitor guy made some comment to one of his coworkers and started the belt again. When the torch emerged from the machine, the belt stopped again. The monitor guy jumped down from his perch and moved toward the torch lying in its bed of coats.

As he approached the torch, I said to him, "That's the Olympic torch. I ran with it yesterday, and I am taking it back to Denver. Would you like to hold it?" I thought taking an offensive position (a good offense is the best defense) would be the best tactic, and it worked!

"Yes," he said and picked it up gently as several of his coworkers gathered around him. They all took turns holding it. A camera appeared, and pictures were taken. Meanwhile, all the torch-holding and picture-taking had stopped the line and created a bit of a commotion.

Unfortunately, the gathering and the work stoppage caught the attention of a little man in a blue coat. He was some kind of supervisor who took his job very seriously.

As the security folks were taking pictures with the torch, the man in the blue coat marched up to them and demanded to know what they were doing. They explained that the object they were holding was the Olympic torch and that this nice gentleman—pointing to me—was letting them take pictures with it. The little man glared at me. He then told the security personnel that "that thing" was not coming through security and that they needed to get back to work pronto.

I was handed the torch, and the security folks scurried back to their posts. The little man turned to me and again declared that the torch was not going any farther. I reiterated that this, gesturing to the torch, was the Olympic torch that I had just run with it the previous day and that I was taking it back home to Denver. Without taking a breath, I told him, "I have been assured by three different sources that it would not be a problem to take the torch through security." I then asked if he wanted to hold the torch, hoping that my tactic would work again. He declined and once again sternly told me that I would not be taking the torch any farther.

I was losing patience, and Ann was becoming concerned. It looked like this was going to be a protracted discussion, so I asked Ann to take the boys to the gate, and I would meet them there. She reluctantly took the kids and left.

Without Ann and the boys watching, I turned my full attention to the little man in the blue coat. I sternly said that I was taking the torch to the plane. In retrospect, this was a poor strategy. I was challenging the little man's authority, and as I spoke those dumb words, the little man literally lunged at me, grabbing the torch from my hands.

I immediately backed off. Realizing my strategic mistake, I reformulated a more personal approach and said, "This torch means a lot to me. I would like to take it back to my home in Colorado." My soft tones emphasized my earnestness and trustworthiness. The man in the blue coat was not impressed.

Despite my personal pleadings, the little man continued to scrutinize the torch. I saw his eyes latch on to the top of the torch where the glass was smudged with Olympic flame soot. I sensed he was going to do something I didn't want to see happen and said, "Please, whatever you do, do not stick your finger into the top of the torch where the soot from the flame is. The soot is special, as it represents the remnants of the flame itself." I thought that perhaps going a little Zen would work on him. It didn't. No sooner than I had finished my little speech, he stuck his stubby finger into the soot. His fingerprint can be seen on the torch to this day.

Now I was mad.

I asked him what I needed to do to end this standoff. He told me I had two choices: 1) leave the torch with him, or 2) throw it away. I told him I didn't like either choice and suggested he give me back the torch and I would go back to the other side of security.

I've found through my years of traveling, if at first someone says no, just keep asking other people. Eventually someone will say yes.

I figured that if I could just get the torch back, I could find another way, someone else to help me get through another security line, where a different security contractor might have a different outlook, and then make my way to the plane.

The little man said I could go back through security. He handed me the torch, and I walked back to the non-secure side. I pondered where to go next.

As I stood there, an older African American airport worker approached me and asked if what I was holding was the Olympic torch. I said that it was. He asked if he could hold it. I gave it to him. He held it proudly. He produced a rag and proceeded to wipe all the fingerprints from the torch handle. He then looked at me and said, "It looks like you had some trouble over there." I said that indeed I had. He glanced around slyly and said, "I think I can help you. Just hold on a minute." He handed me back the torch and disappeared back behind a door.

As I stood there waiting for my new friend's return, a group of blue-coated supervisors joined my nemesis, who was now on my side of security. They gathered about ten yards from me to talk, intermittently pointing at me.

After a few minutes, the elderly gentleman returned and told me that he had "fixed" things. He said, "Good luck," and disappeared once again behind the door. The blue-coat mob continued to grow, and their gestures became more intimidating. I grew more concerned. My inclination was to leave immediately, but my new friend said he'd fixed it, so I decided to wait it out for a few minutes.

Moments later, from down the concourse, I heard the distinct sound of marching. The rhythmic cadence was coming my way. From around a corner I saw them: two seven-foot-tall US Marines, both carrying M-16s. Okay, they weren't really seven feet tall, but they were big, and they were carrying M-16s. I took a glimpse at the band of blue coats. They appeared giddy, so there was no way this was a good thing for me. The Marines marched right to me and stopped.

They asked, "Are you the man with the Olympic torch?"

Well, of course I was. I was the only one in the terminal holding a torch. But I was in no situation to be sarcastic, so I politely and respectfully replied, "Yes, I am."

They said, "You need to come with us." They flanked me and began their march past the blue coats and back toward security.

I thought I was dead. Well, I knew they probably weren't going to kill me, but this was a surreal moment. Had I finally pushed too far?

My genuine concern was quickly alleviated when, as we passed the blue coats, one of the Marines leaned over to me and said, "It's okay. We're here to help you get through security."

I love Marines.

We marched up to the security area and walked right through. Sirens went off—they were carrying guns, after all. Once through, they saluted me and told me to have a nice flight.

I managed a thank-you and began to walk down the concourse to the gate when I heard a familiar voice where it should not have been. I stopped and looked back toward the non-secure part of security to see Ann. She had the little man in the blue coat by the collar and was insisting that he tell her what he had done to her husband.

What was I to do? There was no way the Marines were going to save me again. At that moment, I thought this was a lost cause, but again from down the concourse, I heard the sound of marching feet. This was not the march of Marines. This was the distinctive march of a woman in high heels coming my way with purpose.

Within moments I picked the woman out of the crowd, and her eyes were locked onto me. As she approached, she asked me,

"Why are you not on your way to the gate?" I said that I had been, but my wife—pointing to Ann—was now over there. I pointed to the non-secure side and explained that I needed her to be with me.

The woman sighed deeply, shook her head, and went through security. She grabbed Ann's arm, ripping it from the collar of the little man, walked her through security, and delivered her to me with the command, "Get to the gate now!"

We did as she commanded and made it back to Denver without further incident.

The lesson here is that I knew my map, I knew what I wanted—to take my torch home to Denver. I had a purpose, and I kept pedaling to get where I needed to go. There were definitely obstacles in my path, but I kept the wheels moving forward. I did have to change directions a few times, but I kept some momentum and stayed true to my map.

Unfortunately, we have all seen people who, when faced with a roadblock, just stop pedaling. They throw their hands in the air and just give up. That's

> Nothing in this world can take the place of persistence. Talent will not; nothing is more common than unsuccessful people with talent. Genius will not; unrewarded genius is almost a proverb. Education will not; the world is full of educated failures. Persistence and determination alone are omnipotent.
>
> —CALVIN COOLIDGE

not the plan for success. In so many ways, we have to emulate a shark. They have to keep in constant motion to keep water flowing through their gills; if they don't, they die. It's the same for us.

I have had a few low points, from the bike accident to getting fired, but I have kept riding because I don't know what could be over the next hill. While there may be nothing, there could be something great. You just don't know until you get there, so you have to keep pedaling forward. You have to keep riding and stay true to your map.

God put us on this earth to learn and grow. We do that by pedaling our bikes, consistently moving forward, and staying true to ourselves.

As we pedal forward, it is important that we keep our principles and beliefs in sight. While it's okay to change direction and take a new path, it is not okay to change your values. That's why you need a brand architecture, as I discussed earlier. Before the obstacles appear, you need to know what you stand for. Figuring out your values in the heat of battle won't work; there will be too many temptations to compromise.

Let me share the map I use so I don't get distracted and stop pedaling forward:

- Always treat people with dignity and respect. You should work with people just as you would want to be treated. It's the golden rule for a reason. It's hard to follow this value at times, especially when you feel you have been wronged. But I believe in karma; a wrong will always come back to you.
- Great relationships—whether they are personal or brand relationships—must live in the heart, not the head. Lasting value is emotional, not transactional. Emotional connections keep relationships alive. Consumers buy emotionally then justify logically. So do spouses.
- Everything you do should have a purpose. You should be very clear why you are doing something. If the purpose isn't clear and doesn't pedal you forward, don't do it.
- Always seek to understand. Be a private eye, always interested in finding out what those around you need. Great marketing starts with a clear understanding of how the brand delivers value to the consumer. Great relationships are the same way. Maintain an ongoing

understanding—and interest in understanding—those who you are in a relationship with.

- *Brand* and *life* should be verbs, not nouns. The strength of a brand and the altitude your life obtains is based upon activity. And not just any activity—valued activity. Brands and people cannot be silent. We have to be known for the way we conduct ourselves.

- You are only going to be as good on the outside as you are on the inside. For people, it's living a life full of hope and charity; for brands, it's about having a significant reason for being.

These values are simple and proven. No matter what direction my bike goes, I will adhere to these values.

From a business perspective, in addition to these values, there are five simple questions that should always be asked to keep things on track. Like everything else that is proven and timeless, these are simple, common-sense questions, and they guide the way I manage.

One note of caution: let's not get confused between managing and leadership here. Management is about process; leadership is about inspiration, which there is no process for.

When I make a management decision, I insist on following these simple questions in this important order.

In today's world no one has time for nice-to-do projects. In

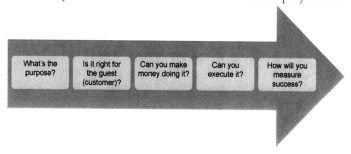

What's the purpose? | Is it right for the guest (customer)? | Can you make money doing it? | Can you execute it? | How will you measure success?

business and in life, everything we do should have a purpose, and we should have some measure for understanding if we accomplished our task or not.

The degree to which you persecute these questions and follow the answers they provide will dictate success. Failure, like in all things, comes most often when you try to shortcut the principles and take the easier road. Adherence to this process or any set of management rules will help you keep your values in place even when you might have to change direction on your bike. When changing direction, it's important to know your map so you don't get lost.

Lesson 10
Find the Joy

What I have learned over the course of my rides is that you can't take one moment for granted. You can't take any time off. Even when our own situation seems dire, I believe it's our obligation to find joy, to find ways to serve others, to reduce others' burdens, and to do it with a smile. When you find this joy, your ride is going to get a lot easier.

Once Ken and I arrived at the emergency room after our accident, in the chaos of that time and place, I learned this great lesson.

As I heard the emergency room doctor assigned to me talking about his concern that perhaps my injuries were too serious to recover from, I became very frightened. In fact, I felt a literal wave of fear swell at my feet and flood over my body. It felt just like a wave, exactly like you'd feel as you lay on a beach and let the waves lap over you.

My recollections during this time are crystal clear, and I recall that my fear was intense. Once those waves of fear washed over my body, it soaked into me and penetrated me to the core.

I was afraid I was going to die. I wasn't ready to go. If I died, I was going to go to hell. You can only imagine the panic that churns within you with that kind of revelation.

As this fear consumed me, my vision turned to what you see in the movies. I know this sounds like a cliché, but I truly saw my life unfold in front of me. Really. Many people have reported that as they were dying, their life flashed in front of them. In my case that really did happen. The focus of my life's movie targeted my fear—my selfishness. This selfishness was bundled not in the sins of commission but the sins of omission—the things I had not done, the moments I had taken for granted, the moments I had not appreciated, the moments I had not been a servant, the moments when I had not sought joy.

> Find a place inside where there's joy, and the joy will burn out the pain.
>
> —Joseph Campbel

So what is this elusive joy?

Is it just the pleasurable emotion you get by the acquisition of some kind of success?

I'm sure it is that, but I have come to understand it's also something much bigger.

I believe strongly that joy is the assurance that God is in control of all the details of our life, that joy is the quiet confidence that ultimately everything is going to be all right, and that this joy can be magnified as we fulfill our measure on this earth. Joy comes to us when we understand that we are doing all we can to help others and ourselves in times of plenty and in times of want. There is joy in service.

As I lay in the emergency room and the waves of guilt washed over me, I clearly saw the instances when I had not helped someone, the times I had not shared a "thank you" or "I love you," the times I had not been of service.

These were occasions when I had not sought joy.

These were powerful and painful memories, memories just as deadly as the sins of commission, but these were simple sins of omission, the sins of carelessness and self-absorption.

My revelation that I was deeply guilty of these sins of omission led to a frank discussion with my Heavenly Father. I sought forgiveness and reconciliation. After some additional painful self-revelation about my shortcomings, I felt forgiveness and redemption. As I did, the waves of guilt that had started this process receded. I felt peace.

After this frightening encounter and several months in the hospital to observe my surroundings, I began to see the power of joy in the patients around us. Those patients who looked beyond themselves, who had kind words that worked to make the best of a bad situation, carried with them a presence. It was joy, and it was accompanied by smiles and laughter. It became clear to me that when you choose to be happy and serve others, it's hard to contain joy.

Ken and I saw a lot of suffering in the hospital. But it became evident to us very quickly there was power in being joyful and wearing a smile.

I have no clinical basis for this observation other than we saw those people who smiled, who laughed, who worked hard to make a negative into a positive, those who were kind to the other patients and their nurses, get better and get out of the hospital. Finding joy was a great healer.

On the other hand, we saw those with nasty, surly demeanors languish in the hospital and do all they could to make others miserable as well.

Ken and I chose to be happy. We had lots of friends and family to help us in this regard. As a result, we made rapid progress and got out of the hospital much faster than expected.

Finding joy is not just a recipe for getting out of the hospital in record time. It is a requirement and a true principle for finding success and happiness in life and work. We are always happier when we are striving to help others. Looking for joy by serving others is not a complicated formula for a happy life, but it is hard to do when so many opposing forces confront us. There are no secret tricks other than to be resolute in seeking to always smile and look for ways to serve others. Finding joy makes life better.

Pizza Hut's great success in the early eighties was built on this concept of joy by serving others. The Pizza Hut community wanted to have fun and did so in many ways by giving back to the community. This service extended to Ken and me as we recovered.

At the headquarters on Douglas Avenue, there was a great deal of discussion about our recovery. I have already shared that nearly daily updates on our condition and progress were issued system-wide. But our coworkers wanted to do more than just read about our recovery. They wanted to participate in it. As a result, there was a Pizza Hut party sign-up sheet where friends at work would be assigned to bring joy to our hospital room.

Because of this organization, we had a constant, scheduled flow of visitors who brought their optimism and good cheer—not to mention toys to get us into trouble. Silly string was a favorite. Our room was covered in it on multiple occasions. These kinds of service, visits, and childlike pranks provided a significant diversion and opportunity to laugh deeply.

The point is, even though we were in a serious way, we had friends take time to serve us, to bring us happiness, and help us smile, laugh, and celebrate life. As a result we all enjoyed great joy.

Businesses need service to grow. Individuals need joy to be healthy.

Many of the most successful companies include service and the pursuit of joy for their employees as part of the DNA and part of their brand architecture.

Smashburger is one of these companies. When building this company from the ground up, it was important to us that there was a strong sense of community and giving back as part of the company culture. It was important enough to include in the original brand architecture. In the company's original book, we wrote:

> Modern brands must have a soul; not only for the products they sell but for the communities in which they live and work. They must have an eye for both local and global citizenship. As our guests enjoy a better burger, we should provide opportunities for them (and us) to give in mind, body, and spirit.

If finding joy is not part of your life today, make a change. If a burger restaurant can make the pledge to find joy, so can you.

Whether it's work or our life's journeys, we need to find joy on our ride. No matter how tough things can be, we need to learn to find some joy in the moment, even if that joy is knowing that the moment will soon be over. We need to search out something in each day, in each ride, to cherish. We need to find ways to serve, even if it is sitting up and creating a better draft for a friend who is suffering on the ride. Find ways to serve and joy will follow.

Without joy life becomes a string of unhappy events, and we as humans will not fulfill our existence. I have always appreciated the important declaration in one of my favorite children's books, *Dinotopia*: "Breathe deep, fly high, seek peace."

I am convinced that when you do, you will find the joy.

Part III

There Is Never
a Finish Line

Keep Pedaling

That's it, the ten life and business lessons I have learned on my bike. Clearly these lessons are not necessarily new to humankind, but I have learned them and relearned them with a lot of sweat, some blood, and some wonderful adventures along the way. Hopefully in some small way, they have reinforced some of the important truths you already knew and have brought a smile or perhaps a grimace to your face as you were reminded of them.

I will end exactly where I started. I wrote this more for me and my progeny than anyone else. I hope over the years that they will find some direction in these lessons. I hope others can also find some direction as well.

All of these lessons really boil down to a couple of realizations: The reality is that we will all have challenges. Our job as humans is to embrace them, love them, and give them purpose. This leads to the second summary point and the title of the book: *Pedal Forward.* After we have learned to love our challenges, we

> Come what may, and love it.
>
> —JOSEPH B. WIRTHLIN

must pedal forward. If we stand still, we will, as Ken wrote in his foreword, be defined by our challenges, not refined by them.

While I have been trying to focus on these principles for some time now, I find that it is a necessity to ask myself constantly if I am living the ten lessons. We are imperfect beings. We are easily led onto paths that we should not follow. We have to be diligent to keep to our most positive path. It's why we go to church. It's why we seek out positive people in our lives. It's why we invest our time in books like this.

To keep on my positive path, I find myself constantly and consciously filing through the ten lessons in my head. I am always asking myself:

- Am I getting up after getting knocked down?
- Am I fully appreciating all aspects of my life—the good and the bad?
- Am I pushing through when times are tough and not taking the easy path?
- Am I using the tools I have been given to focus on what is important?
- Am I staying true to my personal brand architecture, and do I use the principles of brand architecture to make sure the businesses I have responsibility for are staying true to the mission and vision for the brand?
- Am I living a life of action vs. inaction?
- Am I taking the time to celebrate accomplishments? Do I share my thanks enough with those I live and work with?
- Am I communicating effectively? Does everyone who needs to know something know it and do they know it in a timely fashion?
- Am I associating with the best and brightest?
- Am I participating in the economy of deflection in any way, even in small ways?

- Am I staying true to my principles and never compromising?
- And am I finding the joy in all aspects of my life?

Inevitably, during these personal interventions, I find that in some mostly small ways, I have begun to veer from my path. By constant assessing, I can recalibrate and get back to where I need to be.

There is never a finish line. You'll never cross some imaginary line and say, "I'm done. I can stop now." As long as we are breathing, we will not be finished working to keep ourselves on our positive path.

I have had and continue to have a great career because I have put my faith in these ten lessons. After the experience of getting fired, I did not waver in my belief in these principles. It is exactly because I have lived these principles that I have my current job. Rick Schaden, whom I mentioned in an earlier chapter, called a few months into my sabbatical to check in on me. This initial call resulted in a number of discussions, which led to my current position as president of Consumer Concept Group, a restaurant development group.

The ten lessons I have learned on my bike have worked for me. I live these lessons in my own life—every day.

It has been twenty years since the accident knocked me off my bike and bloodied me a bit. The lessons learned that day and since have helped me overcome trials and revel in the joys of my life.

I am still on the bike nearly every day. I still find joy in the ride. I chose to pedal forward.

About the Author

Trey Hall is a twenty-eight-year business veteran who has worked at world-class organizations PepsiCo, Boston Market, Quiznos, Smashburger, Consumer Capital Partners, and TGI Friday's. Trey is currently president of Denver-based Consumer Concept Group, a restaurant-centric direct development firm that creates, opens, and operates modern signature restaurants. He has also helped nonprofit organizations Millennium Promise (dedicated to ending extreme poverty in sub-Saharan Africa) and America's Road Home (dedicated to ending family homelessness in the United States) build their consumer infrastructure.

After earning his undergraduate degree from Brigham Young University, Trey went on for a master's degree from Northwestern University's Medill School of Journalism, where he was recently inducted into the Hall of Achievement.

The author has shared his bike stories and the lessons he has learned from them in university, business, and church settings.

Trey lives with his wife of thirty years in Denver, Colorado. He is dedicated to his family, his friends, and his bike.

CPSIA information can be obtained
at www.ICGtesting.com
Printed in the USA
LVOW10s0829050617

536961LV00025B/952/P

9 780989 355541